Genesis to

THIRTY THEMES IN

MW00523002

THE
BIBLE
STUDY
GUIDE

THE BIBLE STUDY.ORG

THE BIBLE STUDY GUIDE

thebiblestudy.org

The Bible Study Guide: Genesis to Revelation in 30 Lessons

Copyright © 2017 by The Bible Study Organization.
All rights reserved.
King, Robin R.
ISBN 978-1-947841-06-2
Third printing.

Published by The Bible Study Organization
www.thebiblestudy.org

Scriptures unless otherwise cited are from *the Bible, English Standard Version.*

Printed in the United States of America.

CONTENTS

	Foreword		4
	Introduction		5
1	**The Creator, Creation and Fall**	Genesis 1-11	13
2	**Covenant and Lineage**	Genesis 12-50	21
3	**Bondage, Freedom and Law**	Exodus	29
4	**Sin, Sacrifice and Holiness**	Leviticus	37
5	**Organization, Trials and Testing**	Numbers	45
6	**Discipline and Obedience**	Deuteronomy	53
7	**Conquering and Conquests**	Joshua	61
8	**Justice and Deliverance**	Judges, Ruth	69
9	**Governments of God and Man**	1, 2 Samuel, 1 Chronicles	77
10	**Man's Destruction and Exile**	1, 2 Kings, 2 Chronicles	85
11	**Return, Rebuild, Reform and Restore**	Ezra, Nehemiah, Esther, Job	93
12	**Worship, Wisdom, Preaching and Song**	Psalms, Prov., Eccles., Songs	101
13	**Pointing to Christ, Judgment and Peace**	Isaiah	109
14	**Pointing to Failure and Future**	Jeremiah, Lam., Ezekiel., Dan.	117
15	**Pointing to Hope and Promise**	Hosea – Malachi	125
16	**The Savior, Son of God**	Matthew	133
17	**The Savior, Son of Man**	Mark	141
18	**The Risen Lord is our Savior Redeemer**	Luke	149
19	**Salvation is for Believers**	John	157
20	**The Holy Spirit and the Church**	Acts	165
21	**Justification**	Romans	173
22	**Christian Love**	1, 2 Corinthians	181
23	**By Grace through Faith**	Galatians, Ephesians	189
24	**Joy in Knowing Christ**	Philippians, Colossians	197
25	**Waiting for Christ**	1, 2 Thessalonians	205
26	**Gifts and Leadership**	1, 2 Timothy, Titus, Philemon	213
27	**Faith**	Hebrews	221
28	**Sanctification and Good Works**	James, 1, 2 Peter	229
29	**Discerning Truth**	1, 2, 3 John, Jude	237
30	**Glorification and Overcoming Evil**	Revelation	245
	Appendices		253
	Acknowledgements		258

FOREWORD

BY DR. LUDER G. WHITLOCK

To read the Bible is a good thing and a blessing. To know the Bible is far better but seldom achieved. It doesn't have to be that way and your participation in this 30-lesson overview of the Bible is a fine way to remedy that deficiency.

The Bible is God's word. It is a compilation of a collection of books into one that explains who God is and how you got here. It provides the information necessary for your redemption so that if you respond to its message in faith, you can be assured of everlasting life. As God's word, it is the final authority for what you believe and how you live, so you cannot afford to neglect its message any more than you can afford to neglect the fine print in a contract you sign.

One reason for mastering an overview of the Bible is that it enables you to understand the grand narrative and, with it, how God has developed His redemptive plan throughout human history, ultimately sending Christ into the world for your salvation. You not only know what happened and why but you have a clearer grasp of what the future holds.

As you know, there are many questions about what the Bible teaches and often disagreements occur among good Christians, not to mention the jibes and challenges from non-believers. When you have the big picture, as you should after completing this series, you will be much better equipped to know how to handle those matters. You will know where to go to find the answers and have a clearer sense of how important those may be in comparison to the whole counsel of God. After all, it is His plan and His message that you must understand if you hope to please Him and the place to begin is through your commitment to get the big picture.

If you are diligent through this overview you will not regret it. You will be in a much better position to serve the Lord knowledgeably and faithfully.

DR. LUDER G. WHITLOCK, JR. is president emeritus of Reformed Theological Seminary and author of the new book, *Divided We Fall: Overcoming a History of Christian Disunity,* (2017). He was executive director of the *Spirit of the Reformation Study Bible* and served on the editorial council of Eternity Advisory board for the *English Standard Version* of *the Bible.*

INTRODUCTION

GENESIS TO REVELATION

God inspires His all-time best-selling book, the Bible, explicitly to relate to His created men, women, boys and girls who bear His image. In it—from the very beginning of earth and creation—He documents the earliest history of His created world, to the Bible's last book which gives us visions of eternity with Him.

Genesis 1 begins, *"In the beginning, God created the heavens and the earth. The earth was without form and void, and darkness was over the face of the deep. And the Spirit of God was hovering over the face of the waters. And God said, 'Let there be light,' and there was light."* Thus began the world. But more importantly, through the Bible God draws all mankind—including you—to Himself through the Light and Word—Jesus Christ. Your Bible includes the world's history, purpose and future.

GOD'S WORD IS A ROADMAP FOR YOUR LIFE

The whole-Bible story is best learned in its order; the themes understood in a contextual building process—from Genesis to Revelation. With this inter-denominational, inductive study, you can learn the major themes with corresponding book names and study many key scripture points that support them.

You might additionally plan to read through the whole Bible—perhaps in a summer—and personally learn the key scriptures for your discussions and memory. The more we learn about our Creator and Savior, the more we want to hear His plan for our lives.

CONSIDER what you know and think about the Bible and God. Do you wish to know more about who created you? What about the possibility of learning more about what God may have planned for you own life? Consider using this opportunity to learn about the Old Testament Father, Creator, Provider, and Sustainer of our forefathers in Christ. Consider how the Father sent His Son, God's second "person" Jesus Christ, to visit earth as your Lord, to teach us in the four Gospels about life eternal, and to offer you salvation in Him. Consider how Jesus promised His disciples the third "person" of God—His Spirit demonstrated in Acts and the Letters—to follow after Him on earth as our Counselor and Guide in this personal salvation. And finally, consider the visions of the eternal Heaven that Christ shows you in Revelation. This adventure is the outline of your whole-Bible study.

You may want to establish personal learning goals for your journey through the Bible using these 30 key themes and corresponding study lessons. These weekly lessons include home-study questions which are the basis for your journal and small-group discussion. Pray, read and complete these questions (based on the English Standard Version), in order to be fully prepared for sharing and learning together.

Following your questions, a summary is provided that ties together the lesson's themes for that book or group of books. Together in a building process, these themes and lessons demonstrate the overall point of what God is doing in that part of history. These steps will strengthen your personal belief and growth. If you are in a class or Bible study group, you should extend your learning through active discussions and in fellowship. This 30-theme lesson Guide is designed for both personal and group studies, in class or small-group settings. It will be a basis for later in-depth studies of each book.

STUDYING THE BIBLE

From the beginning of time God has guided us to learn His words—the basic laws for all times (Deut. 11:18-25). In God's planned timing, Jesus, the Word of God incarnate, completed for us the law (Gal. 4:4) for *"a people prepared,"* (Luke 1:17).

The writer of Hebrews describes the Word as *"living and active, sharper than any two-edged sword,"* (Heb. 4:12). The Bible is the only book that contains living words, can pierce our soul and judge our thoughts, by which all men and women will be judged, and that gives us the keys to eternal life.

Luke records of Jesus, *"Then he opened their minds to understand the Scriptures,"* (Luke 24:45).

Many of us have found the Bible to be somewhat difficult to completely understand on our own, so we depend mainly on others to "tell us about it." Paul says, however, that *"For we are not writing to you anything other than what you read and understand and I hope you will fully understand,"* (2 Cor. 1:13).

Paul thus tells us that God gave us His written word so that we can read it and understand it. In doing so, we can allow the Spirit to use that knowledge to transform our lives. And the value of knowing scripture, Paul told Timothy, is that as you learn you become convinced, receive wisdom, and are led to salvation. The words you read are all inspired by God for teaching, reproof, reform, and equipping mankind for good works (2 Tim. 3:14-17).

Interpretative Principles for Your Study

1. ***Hebrew and Greek***—the Bible Old Testament origins were Hebrew. We speak English and are "Western," like the Greek culture and language. So we tend to think "Greek," missing much of the Eastern-written Hebrew meanings. Hebrew is and was an "Eastern" language like Asian languages today and is written and spoken using illustrations, or word-pictures (e.g., *"the early bird gets the worm"*). Greek is a Western language with concrete, literal and descriptive phrases, like English today (e.g., *"the first person to arrive will have the advantage"*).

2. ***Literary Forms***—writers and early oral "tellers" of the Bible used various literary forms to tell the messages; i.e., poetry, prose, news or journalism, imagery, symbolism, illustrations, etc.

3. ***Literal Interpretation in Context***—literal interpretation of the surrounding context is key to understanding what God is asking us to learn in any specific text. We should follow typical rules of grammar, context, syntax, and literary style, listening for God's explanation and plan.

4. ***Scripture Interprets Scripture***—scripture is not in conflict with scripture, but helps us understand from different perspectives. It is dangerous to attempt to interpret scripture with science, modern history, philosophy, or any other self-driven human work.

5. ***Explicit Interprets the Implicit***—always use the "explained" passage to understand the "implied" passage of the same topic, using scripture for cross-references.

6. ***Limitation Principle***—the Bible does not tell us everything about everything, as science (and our Greek-trained minds) would want. The Bible tells us what God wants us to know, and no more. It focuses on relationships between God, us, and others.

7. ***Historical Principle***—the message should be seen in relation to its context in God's redemptive plan. It is very dangerous to take verses out of their context. A Genesis-to-Revelation study helps us see the narrative message.

8. ***Jesus Christ is the Key***—Jesus said to His followers, *"'These are my words that I spoke to you while I was still with you, that everything written about me in the Law of Moses and the Prophets and the Psalms must be fulfilled.' Then he opened their minds to understand the Scriptures,"* Luke 24:44-45. (See also John 5:39, 46-47.)

THE BIBLE IS A BOOK AND A LIBRARY

The Bible is both one book and a whole library—with a single narrative story. God Himself narrates this 66-book story—which is our history and future with Him. His story is our history and becomes our personal journey. He first appears as our Father in the Old Testament, directly speaking to our patriarchs and prophets who are the inspired writers (see Appendices I-IV, pages 253-255).

In the Gospels God again appears personally in His "second person" as Christ the Son of God who speaks directly and inspires the Gospel writers (see Appendices V and VI, pages 256-257). He acclaims Himself the Messiah King. At the end of the Gospels Christ promises God's "third person" and appears as the Holy Spirit—our Counselor and Guide.

The Old Testament—the first 39 books—are His "preparation" of His earth and man to receive Him personally. The Hebrews writer says, *"Long ago, at many times and in many ways, God spoke to our fathers by the prophets,"* (Heb. 1:1).

The New Testament's 27 books begin with the four Gospels when Christ acclaims Himself the Son of God, Savior, Messiah, King. Acts, and the 22 letters are the "completion" of God's redemptive plan for man. Heb. 1:3 continues, *"but in these last days he has spoken to us by his Son, whom he appointed the heir of all things, through whom also he created the world. He is the radiance of the glory of God and the exact imprint of his nature, and he upholds the universe by the word of his power. After making purification for sins, he sat down at the right hand of the Majesty on high."*

Paul writes, *"But when the fullness of time had come, God sent forth his Son, born of woman, born under the law, to redeem those who were under the law, so that we might receive adoption as sons. And because you are sons, God has sent the Spirit of his Son into our hearts, crying, 'Abba! Father!'"* (Gal. 4:4-6).

Christ says to His apostles, *"I will send him to you. And when he comes, he will convict the world concerning sin and righteousness and judgment: concerning sin, because they do not believe in me; concerning righteousness, because I go to the Father, and you will see me no longer; concerning judgment, because the ruler of this world is judged. 'I still have many things to say to you, but you cannot bear them now. When the Spirit of truth comes, he will guide you into all the truth, for he will not speak on his own authority, but whatever he hears he will speak, and he will declare to you the things that are to come. He will glorify me, for he will take what is mine and declare it to you. All that the Father has is mine; therefore I said that he will take what is mine and declare it to you,'"* (John 16:7b-15).

The final chapter of the Bible, Revelation 22, Jesus concludes the Bible text through John' writing, saying, *"I warn everyone who hears the words of the prophecy of this book: if anyone adds to them, God will add to him the plagues described in this book, and if anyone takes away from the words of the book of this prophecy, God will take away his share in the tree of life and in the holy city, which are described in this book."* He extends his invitation in love saying, *"The Spirit and the Bride say, "Come." And let the one who hears say, "Come." And let the one who is thirsty come; let the one who desires take the water of life without price,"* (Rev. 22:17).

1. Read Deut. 11:18-25—Learning God's Words

From the beginning of time God has guided us to follow His Word and learn His laws for all times. Moses had the responsibility of sharing God's Word with the people of Israel.

a. What are some of the ways they learned His words?

_____

_____

b. How in these times might you benefit from knowing His words?

_____

_____

2. Read 2 Cor. 1:12-14—Understanding God's Words

Paul writes to the Corinthians that *"we write nothing else to you than what you read and understand, and I hope that you will understand to the end."*

a. How does earthly wisdom differ from wisdom that is by the grace of God? (See also Heb. 13:7-9.)

_____

_____

b. What is God's ultimate purpose in Paul's desire for them? What do you think "the day of our Lord Jesus" means?

_____

_____

3. Read 2 Tim. 3:14-17—Continuing in God's Words

The value of knowing scripture, Paul told Timothy, is that as you learn you become convinced, receive wisdom, and are led to salvation.

a. How do you think the Bible might make you *"wise for salvation"*?

_____

_____

b. In what ways do you think knowing Scripture might be useful throughout your life? Why? (See verses 16 and 17.)

_____

_____

THE CREATOR, CREATION AND FALL

GENESIS 1 - 11

The opening of Genesis shows us how such a great and powerful God over the universe begins His relationship with man and woman as His "crown of creation." God made them in His own image and over His perfect creation. But then, their selfish rebellion leads all of mankind into a desperate need for God's forgiveness and redemption.

QUESTIONS FOR PERSONAL THOUGHT AND DISCUSSION

1. Read Gen. 1:1-4 and John 1:1-5, 14—God Is the Triune Creator

a. Who created the heavens and the earth? (See 1:1-2.) Who besides the Spirit was with God at Creation? (See John 1:1-5, 14.)

b. What was the first thing created that the Creator told us was and is "good"? (See 1:3-4.) What did Jesus call Himself in John 8:12? How do we receive goodness and redemption through Jesus?

2. Read Gen. 1:26-29—God Gave Man and Woman Relationship with Himself, Others and Earth

a. Describe God's relationship with man and woman before and after the rebellion. (See 3:8-19 and 5:1-5, 22-23, 32.)

b. Describe God's intended relationship for man with the earth and animals.

3. Read Gen. 2:1-8—Man and Woman Created

a. How did God form man and woman, giving them life? (See also 2:18-23.)

b. What three kinds of trees were in the Garden, cited in verse 9? What two specific trees are cited in verse 9? Which tree is everlasting? (See Rev. 22:1-2.)

c. Which tree is prohibited? (See also 2:15-17.) What does God expect of man? Why? (See also 1:26-27.)

4. Read Gen. 3:1-7 and 4:1-7—Man and Woman Fell into Sin, But Are Promised Redemption

a. What were the root causes of the temptation and fall? (See also 3:13, James 1:12-15 and Rev. 12:7-12.)

b. Why did God "punish" them for disobedience? How might the curse of the serpent have led to the redemption offer for all mankind? (See John 8:44 and Rom. 16:19-20.)

c. What did God offer woman and man as paths toward redemption? (See 3:14-19.) Who is "He" in verse 15?

d. Compare God's sacrificial expectations of Cain and Abel, and their responses (4:1-5). How does sin "crouch at the door?" (See also 1 Peter 5:6-11.)

e. What guidance does God give Cain in verses 6-7? Why?

5. Read Gen. 6:5-22 and 8:20-22—God Saw the Faith of Noah and Gave Redemption

What two things did Noah build? (See 6:14-22 and 8:20-22.) Why did God protect and treat Noah differently than all the rest of mankind? (See Heb. 11:7) Why and how did God treat his family?

6. Read Gen. 9:18-27, 10:6-20, 11:1-9—God Divided Nations and Languages

a. What generational consequences do Shem, Ham, and Japheth illustrate? (See 9:18-27.) What did Ham do that displeased God? How did God respond? (See 10:6-20.) What was the future for Ham's descendants and lands of Canaan, Sodom, Gomorrah, Philistia and Gaza?

b. At the Babel tower, how did men try to be like gods? What did man do before and at the tower? (See 11:4.) What two things did God do?

THE CREATOR, CREATION AND FALL

GENESIS 1-11

God Is the Creator and Light of All

Genesis means "beginning," and introduces the story of God's greatness and mankind's need for redemption that runs throughout the Bible. God demonstrated His creativity, love, mercy and grace from the very beginning. Mankind, representing all men and women, demonstrated rebellion, judgment and need for God's forgiveness. We see immediately in Genesis God's authority over all mankind, over Satan and over evil. And we see His curse for all evil and His plan of mercy and grace to redeem His created men and women.

CONSIDER how God's earliest created man and woman—from the very beginning—were in an innocent relationship with their God. Consider how we each enter life somewhat innocent and totally dependent on our Creator. But like Adam and Eve, we taste of their trees of selfishness, pride, sin and death. However, we can also learn about the tree of life—a redemption plan that God has had from the beginning of time for those who listen to His call and respond. Consider how your Creator offers you this solid basis for hope—hope not in ourselves but in the Creator and Redeemer of our world.

Consider how the tree of life brings Light into your world as you taste of God's original plan for your life and as He redeems you to His image through Jesus Christ.

God is the Creator of all life and all things. He made all of mankind and gave them a world of wonder and beauty in which to live. Man and woman followed Satan's temptation and sinfully rebelled against God and His commandments, leading the world to drown in sin. But God's expelling of Adam and Eve from His garden, the flood, and the Babel-tower destruction still did not separate man from God's mercy and care. God continually called His people back to Him.

All that God had made was good. Nothing that was made by God was or is evil by its design—but rather tempted by Satan to sin (see James 1). Light is the first thing God said is *"good,"* creating day.

Jesus is the world's Light from the very beginning (John 8:12), and the *"Word of God."* Thus, Jesus Christ the Word is referenced in Genesis as the "second person" of the triune God. The apostle John said, *"In the beginning was the Word, and the Word was with God, and the Word was God. He was in the beginning with God. All things were made through him, and without him was not anything made that was made,"* (John 1:1-3).

These words, which remind us of Genesis 1:1, declare that the Creator who appears in the opening chapters of Genesis is Jesus Christ Himself, acting in the days before He *"became flesh and dwelt among us,"* (John 1:14).

Mankind is the Image-bearer of God

Man was created in God's image (Gen. 1:27) and to live in that image. God matched His creation with a people who could relate to it and to Him—He fashioned His own in His image and His likeness (Gen. 5:1-2). God made mankind the crown of His creation, the centerpiece of His earth and His plan. They are called to replenish the earth and subdue it (Gen. 1:28); dress, till and keep it (Gen. 2:15); and exercise dominion over it (Gen. 1:28).

God granted to all men and women, boys and girls, freedom within His limited will. Mankind was never free to exclusively do his own will. As God's creation we are of His ownership, made in His image, and bound by His will. Our freedom is only within God's limits. All bondage in sin is outside of God's will for us. We are dependent on Him to remove all bondage and sin (see Rom 3:23-26).

Man Sinned, Breaking Relationship with God

Man's selfish choices began the fall. However, God promised and began future redemption even as man disobeyed His commands. Brokenness in life always results when relationship—as God designed it—is separated in disobedient sin.

The Hebrew definition of sin is "revolt against God." It is a quest for unrestrained, selfish freedom regardless of God's commands. Sin separates—in broken relationship—God from man. After being tempted, man and woman submitted to selfish sin breaking their relationship with their God their Creator (Gen. 3).

God Cursed Satan and Evil, Promising Redemption for Mankind

God did not abandon His sinful creatures. A new promise was given—a level of power over evil itself. Gen. 3:14 says, *"The Lord God said to the serpent, 'Because you have done this, cursed are you above all livestock and above all beasts of the field; on your belly you shall go, and dust you shall eat all the days of your life. I will put enmity between you and the woman, and between your offspring and her offspring; he shall bruise your head, and you shall bruise his heel.'"*

Good and evil were illustrated by God in both Cain and Abel through comparing their offerings (Gen 4). Cain, illustrating the continued fall of man, didn't offer his first and best to God—as Abel did. Abel did, as we are expected to do today, exhibit relationship with God when he—by faith—brought the *"firstlings and fat portions"* before God. God still sought Cain's heart in telling him *"sin is couching at the door; its desire is for you, but you must master it."*

Good and evil were forever distinguished and separated (Gen. 5-8). God saw that the wickedness of man was great (Gen. 6) and flooded the earth, saving only Noah and his household (Gen. 7), along with each animal species. Noah's sons would repopulate the earth under a covenant between God and the new families. Genesis 6:5-8 says, *"The Lord saw that the wickedness of man was great in the earth, and that every intention of the thoughts of his heart was only evil continually. And the Lord regretted that he had made man on the earth, and it grieved him to his heart. So the Lord said, 'I will blot out man whom I have created from the face of the land, man and animals and creeping things and birds of the heavens, for I am sorry that I have made them.' But Noah found favor in the eyes of the Lord."*

God made a covenant with Noah and mankind to *"never again curse the ground because of man, for the intention of man's heart is evil from his youth. Neither will I ever again strike down every living creature as I have done. While the earth remains, seedtime and harvest, cold and heat, summer and winter, day and night, shall not cease,"* (Gen. 8:21-22). Good was blessed while evil was cursed (Gen. 9-10). Shem honored Noah and God. After Ham shamed Noah, his descendants, becoming Canaan, were cursed by Noah for all generations (Gen. 9:22-26 and 10:15-20). (See Appendix I, page 253.)

Worldwide selfishness was prevented (Gen. 11). Men, all of one language, had become their own gods in uniting to build the tower at "Babel." To prevent all mankind from such selfishness, God separated everyone into ethnic nations of different tongues. Some would listen, honor, and follow Him within His Godly limits, while sin and evil would forever be outside God's sphere and will for His people.

CONSIDER how God began His relationship with man and His perfect creation, providing all that they could want. Their selfish response was to fall into the bondage of sin. Today—we still must choose between self and God, death and life. But He calls for us and yearns for our trust, faith and freedom in Jesus Christ. Consider today your own personal relationship with your Creator!

COVENANT AND LINEAGE

GENESIS 12 - 50

Genesis shows us how the God over the entire universe begins His relationship with His created mankind. As men and women are constantly tempted in sin, they hear directly from their Creator-Redeemer. Beginning with chapter 12, God covenants with men and women an offer of divine relationship, and provides a protected lineage to enact and sustain that relationship leading to life in Christ.

QUESTIONS FOR PERSONAL THOUGHT AND DISCUSSION

1. Read Gen. 12:1-4—God Blessed Abram with a Covenant to be a Blessing to the Whole World

a. What things did God promise all mankind through the covenant with Abram (12:1-3)? What special role did Abram receive? His family?

THE WORLD TO BE BLESSED THROUGH ABRAM

b. Does God really care about His creation? All people? You?

YES, He offers a DEVINE RELATIONSHIP

c. What was Abram's response? (See 12:4) What is our role in this covenant?

HE LISTENED AND TOOK HIS FAMILY AS GOD INSTRUCTED

2. Read Gen. 15:1-6, 18-20 and 16:1-4, 15—Sarai and Abram Disobeyed God

a. Describe God's plan for Sarai and Abram's family. What did Sarai and Abram do outside of God's plan? (See also 17:1-21, 18:9-14.)

b. What is meant by "limited freedom"? Why does God give us limits? (See also Rom. 3:9-12, 19-26.)

c. What names did God change and why? (17:5, 15) How did God use circumcision in His plan of redemption? What similar sign of faith does He use today? (See 1 Peter 3:18-22.)

3. Read Gen. 18:17-26, 19:14-17, 23-29—God Separated His Righteous from the Wicked

a. Why did God separate His lineage from others?

b. What was Sodom's wicked practice? How might that have hurt God's plan for Abraham's family to be a blessing?

4. Read Gen. 21:1-7 and 26:3-6—Abraham and Sarah Bore Isaac, Received God's Blessing

a. How did God's plan with Isaac ultimately succeed over the family's selfish human failings?

b. What roles did Sarai (Sarah), Abram (Abraham), Hagar, Ishmael, and Isaac play? (See 21:12-21, 26:1-5.)

5. Read Gen. 22:1-13—Abraham and Isaac were Faithfully Obedient

a. How did God test Abraham's faith?

b. How did God use Isaac to confirm His covenant promises to Abraham and Sarah? (See also Heb. 11:17-20.)

c. Compare 22:1-13 with Matt. 27:43-50. In each passage, who is the father, the only son, the sacrifice, and the Lamb of God?

6. Read Gen. 30:1-7 and 35:9-12, 22-29—Jacob and the 12 Tribes Were God's Lineage for Blessings

a. How did God's plan unfold for Israel as a nation?

_____

_____

b. How would he use these 12 brothers and their families to advance the covenant? (Read Stephen's summary in Acts 7:1-16.)

_____

_____

c. How did Joseph forgive his brothers? (See 45:4-5.) How did God achieve confession for forgiveness? (See 45:13.)

_____

_____

LESSON 2 SUMMARY

COVENANT AND LINEAGE

GENESIS 12 - 50

God Made a Covenant with Abraham to Bless All the Families of the Earth

God's covenant with Abraham demonstrates God's grace and man's response in faith. Regeneration of man—in relation to God—is dependent on God's will for man in this ever-unfolding covenant. The Abrahamic covenant was given in Gen. 12:1-3 and ratified in 15:1-21.

Gen. 12:1-4 reads, *"Now the Lord said to Abram, "Go from your country and your kindred and your father's house to the land that I will show you. And I will make of you a great nation, and I will bless you and make your name great, so that you will be a blessing. I will bless those who bless you, and him who dishonors you I will curse, and in you all the families of the earth shall be blessed." So Abram went, as the Lord had told him, and Lot went with him. Abram was seventy-five years old when he departed from Haran."*

CONSIDER how God first created mankind—in His own image and in an innocent relationship with their Creator. But after many years and generations of mankind's sinfulness God was ready to unfold an everlasting redemption plan for those who would listen to Him and respond. God chose Abraham to birth not only a family, but a nation and lineage of Jesus Christ who brings eternal Light into our world. Because of God's grace and Abraham's faithfulness the whole earth can know a

Savior. With Abraham's stories you can appreciate even more the special relationship God offers those who hear, believe, and are faithful and obedient.

God promised to Israel, first, great land (Gen. 12:1 and 15:18), second, a great name and nation (Gen.12:2, 13:16), and third, a great blessing for the whole world (Gen. 12:3). But even with God's promise, the nomadic family struggled. To protect the plan, God separated Abraham from his nephew Lot, who had prospered in the evil city Sodom (Gen. 13). Sarah, 90 years old, distrusted God's plan of having children, and turned to Hagar, her maid, to bear Ishmael to Abraham. This infidelity to God and His plan show Sarah's and Abraham's weakened trust in their God. But God persisted in His faithfulness.

God Promised Isaac as Lineage for the Blessing

Abraham and Sarah both laughed at the thought of bearing the son God promised. Genesis 17:17-19 reads, *"Then Abraham fell on his face and laughed and said to himself, 'Shall a child be born to a man who is a hundred years old? Shall Sarah, who is ninety years old, bear a child?' And Abraham said to God, 'Oh that Ishmael might live before you!' God said, 'No, but Sarah your wife shall bear you a son, and you shall call his name Isaac. I will establish my covenant with him as an everlasting covenant for his offspring after him.'"*

Abraham's Family Was Protected, United and Separated to God

God and Abraham protected the family, and initially protected Lot (Gen. 13) and the evil city Sodom from God's wrath (Gen. 18). But when Abraham's lineage was threatened, God ultimately protected the plan by saving only Lot in the final destruction of Sodom and Gomorrah (Gen. 19). God changed Abram's name to Abraham, marked him with circumcision, and gave him Sarah's promised son— Isaac—who was circumcised by God's command (Gen. 21). With Isaac's birth, God's plan unfolded with His chosen lineage.

God Tested Abraham's Obedience and Faith

Genesis 22 illustrates God's test of Abraham's obedient faith. He asked him to take his *"only son Isaac"* whom he loved, and offer him as a sacrifice. Abraham obeyed in faith God's command, preparing to slay his son. Verses 11-12 say, *"But the angel of the Lord called to him from heaven and said, 'Abraham, Abraham!' And he said, 'Here I am.' He said, 'Do not lay your hand on the boy or do anything to him, for now I know that you fear God, seeing you have not withheld your son, your only son, from me.'"* Then God provided a sacrificial lamb for Abraham to offer as his offering instead of his son. This is the same faithful God who offered His only Son a Sacrifice in our stead.

Jacob and Esau Were Born to Isaac and Rebekah

Isaac and his wife Rebekah also were barren and prayed for children. God answered with twins named Jacob and Esau (Gen. 25). As a young man, Jacob once convinced his twin brother Esau, tired and famished after a day of hunting, to trade his first-born inheritance for Jacob's freshly cooked pottage. Esau agreed to the trade. When Isaac, old and blind, prepared to transfer the family inheritance to Esau, his first born, his wife Rebekah schemed with Jacob to pretend he instead was Esau. The scheme worked and God honored Esau's mistake. Jacob inherited the birthright as God used a sinful act for good.

Jacob Began the Twelve Tribes' Origin

The roots of God's organizational plan developed within Abraham's family. His son Isaac, and Isaac's son Jacob formed the lineage (Gen. 30). Jacob had two wives—sisters Leah and Rachel—because of their father's insistence on giving his oldest daughter first. Jacob had picked Rachel, the younger, but received both as wives, as well as their maids Bilhah and Zilpah. Jacob had six sons with Leah, two sons with Rachel, Joseph and Benjamin, two sons with Bilhah, and two sons with Zilpah. These 12 sons (Gen. 35:23-26) formed the 12 tribes. God blessed Jacob, changed his name to Israel, and said, *"I am God Almighty: be fruitful and multiply. A nation and a company of nations shall come from you,"* (Gen. 35:11). (See Appendix I, page 253.)

Joseph Became a Remnant of Israel in Egypt

Genesis 37:3-4 says, *"Now Israel loved Joseph more than any other of his sons, because he was the son of his old age. And he made him a robe of many colors. But when his brothers saw that their father loved him more than all his brothers, they hated him and could not speak peacefully to him."* His brothers conspired to kill him, but resorted instead to sell him to Ishmaelites as a slave to be sold to Egypt (Gen. 37). The Lord was with Joseph and he became successful, prospered, and was made overseer of all that Pharaoh had in Egypt (Gen. 39).

Back in Canaan, Joseph's family was struggling from a national famine. The brothers came to Egypt to buy grain (Gen. 42), and saw Joseph. Genesis 45:3-5 says, *"And Joseph said to his brothers, 'I am Joseph! Is my father still alive?' But his brothers could not answer him, for they were dismayed at his presence. So Joseph said to his brothers, 'Come near to me, please.' And they came near. And he said, 'I am your brother, Joseph, whom you sold into Egypt. And now do not be distressed or angry with yourselves because you sold me here, for God sent me before you to preserve life.'"*

While the lineage of Israel in Canaan suffered in the famine (Gen. 47), Joseph—the remnant of Israel in Egypt—flourished. God had used the evil act of slavery for good. In a covenant act of forgiveness, Joseph said to them, *"'Do not fear, for am I in the place of God? As for you, you meant evil against me, but God meant it for good, to bring it about that many people should be kept alive, as they are today. So do not fear; I will provide for you and your little ones.' Thus he comforted them and spoke kindly to them,"* (Gen. 50:19-21).

CONSIDER how God had a plan that was bigger than the actions of men. Joseph's brothers meant evil, but God used their actions for good, and Joseph forgave his brothers in God's grace and plan. Think about how this final act of Christ-like forgiveness and the enduring kingdom of God completes Genesis with profound victory and promise! Praise God for His covenant of forgiveness!

BONDAGE, FREEDOM AND LAW

EXODUS

God, in a rescue act complete with drama and thrill, in Exodus leads His people out of sinful captivity—bondage—toward a promised place of freedom, justice and protection. After 400 years of bondage in Egypt, Israel was ready to leave the chains of slavery and seek its covenant-promised homeland as a new, holy nation of God.

QUESTIONS FOR PERSONAL THOUGHT AND DISCUSSION

1. Read Ex. 1:1-14 and 2:23-3:12—Israel Was Strong but Cried Out Under Egypt's Bondage

a. How did Israel's bondage and cries to God make them stronger? (See 1:11-14 and 2:23.)

_____

_____

b. Read 2:1-14. As God protected His lineage in Egypt, how did God use the evil king's daughter for good? Why Moses? (See 3:1-12.)

_____

_____

2. Read Ex. 4:1-12—Moses Gave Excuses While God Persisted and Equipped Him for the Exodus

a. What were Moses' excuses? (See 4:1, 10.)

_____

_____

b. What were God's three miracles, or "signs," for Moses to use to convince his detractors? (See 4:2-9.)

_____

_____

3. Read Ex. 6:1-13, 7:1-6—God Promised Deliverance and Cursed Egypt with Ten Plagues

a. God cursed Egypt with plagues even as He blessed Israel (Scan 7-11). How do these events fulfill the covenant with Abraham? (Read Gen. 12:3 and compare Ex. 12:12-13.)

_____

_____

b. As Moses pleaded to Pharaoh, *"Let my people go,"* Pharaoh was warned and briefly repented for Egypt before God (9:27-35). Do you think God hardens people's hearts? If so, how?

_____

_____

c. How did God "pass over" and save His chosen followers?
    (See 12:12-13, 29-30 and 13:17-14:4.)

_____

_____

4. Read Ex. 12:1-7 and 16:1-7—Freedom Was Given for Israel and Passover Commemorated

a. Compare the Passover in Egypt to God's sacrifice and
    memorial for our salvation in Christ's death. (Compare
    12:26-28, 43-50 with 1 Cor. 11:23-26.)

_____

_____

b. When God fought off Israel's enemies and they were
    devoured by the Red Sea, what was Israel's response in
    14:31 and 15:1-18? What is your favorite line in the song?

_____

c. How did future generations remember God's protection and
    deliverance at the Red Sea? (See Josh. 4:19-24.)

_____

5. Read Ex. 15:22-27, 16:4-8—The People Complain

a. How many days into "freedom" did the people complain of
    thirst? What did God provide and what were His "tests"?

_____

b. In 16:4-8, what did God provide the people for their hunger and how did they respond? What lessons were they learning from God?

6. Read Ex. 18:8-23; 19:5-8; 20:1-20— Judges and Laws were Instituted for Justice and Order

a. When Moses told Jethro about God's provisions, the peoples' disputes, and their interests in God, what was Jethro's reaction to God's faithfulness? (See 18:12.)

b. What was Jethro's advice for statutes, laws, justice and peace? (See 18:19-23.)

c. Compare the first nine Commandments (20:1-16) to the tenth (20:17). What is different about the tenth that makes it less visible and less accountable to others, and thus harder?

d. What three purposes does Moses tell the people about God's laws? (See 20:20.) Compare Christ's purposes for today (See 1 Tim. 1:8-11 and Rom. 3:19-20.)

LESSON 3 SUMMARY

BONDAGE, FREEDOM AND LAW

EXODUS

God Delivered Israel from Bondage and Sin

God, in an offer of covenant redemption, led His people out of sinful captivity—bondage—toward a promised place of freedom, protection, justice and provision. After 400 years of bondage in Egypt, Israel was ready to leave the chains of slavery and seek its covenant-promised homeland. Moses, God's appointed deliverer, announced the ten plagues of Egyptian judgment, and then led God's people toward their holy land. Moses recounted their exodus from bondage (Ex.1-18), and then related the instructions given by God on Mount Sinai for the civilization and worship of this young, holy nation (Ex. 19-40).

CONSIDER how God gives us both freedom in Christ and many responsibilities that go with it. Along with this new freedom from Egypt's bondage, God's people needed to recognize their own sin against Him and others. They were being offered the means to re-create the relationship God designed and always intended for mankind, and to develop a world where people can come to know God through His covenant relationship. Consider how the laws and statutes we learn and obey in our own communities allow us to participate in wholesome peace.

Consider how the laws God gave Israel—the Ten Commandments as well as commands to sacrifice to God in place of sin—give us even greater peace with our world and Creator.

God's redemption of his nation Israel began with the Passover—all of the firstborn of Egypt died, but those of Israel were "passed over" and saved. God's protection continued with the Red Sea crossing and His blessings of memorials (Ex. 12), direction (Ex. 13), protection (Ex. 14), sustenance (Ex. 16), justice (Ex. 17-19), and laws (Ex 20).

God was uniting His people for their strength and growth as the new covenant nation. Circumcision, instituted in Gen. 17, was now remembered as an outward, physical and permanent sign of their inward commitment and faithful heart. Separation was sometimes provided by God to protect His people. Tribal separation, separation within families, and geographic separation had already been taught as sometimes necessary, as illustrated in Genesis. Israel often found itself separated from others, to God. Covenant promises were remembered from generation to generation within the tribes of Israel.

Egypt's Bondage Strengthened Israel

Egypt's tightly-bound oppression actually strengthened Israel's numbers and abilities, from 70 people to millions of God-fearing believers. Ex. 1:12-14 reads, *"But the more they were oppressed, the more they multiplied and the more they spread abroad. And the Egyptians were in dread of the people of Israel. So they ruthlessly made the people of Israel work as slaves and made their lives bitter with hard service, in mortar and brick, and in all kinds of work in the field. In all their work they ruthlessly made them work as slaves."*

God protected His holy lineage with Moses' birth. He prepared the nation for freedom and prepared Egypt for His wrath on those who would curse His people. God saw Israel's burdens and felt their pain when they cried out to Him. He appeared to Moses as an angel at the burning bush, ready to call him to lead His people out of bondage.

Moses Gave Excuses but Accepted God's Call

Moses gave excuses to God saying he could not represent Israel to Pharaoh. Once Moses accepted the Lord's will for him to lead Israel against the Pharaoh's bondage, God cast plagues over Egypt (Ex. 7-11) as pressure on Pharaoh to take God seriously. In this new position of power, as the Egyptian Pharaoh knew Moses' God was stronger than Egypt, Moses began to ask him to *"Let my people go!"* (Ex. 8).

Pharaoh's heart was hardened by God's persistence with the plagues, but he briefly repented acknowledging his sin (Ex. 9). Pharaoh went back on his word, again hardened his heart to the Lord, and more plagues persisted against Egypt. Finally God instituted the death plague against all the first-born of Egypt, "passing over" the Israelites in an act of covenant protection and freedom (Ex. 12).

God Freed Israel from Bondage

Moses led the people out of Egypt, with God protecting them *"by day in a pillar of cloud...and by night in a pillar of fire,"* (Ex. 13), and across the parted Red Sea (Ex. 14). The Egyptians, following them, were consumed in the waters. As much as Israel wanted its freedom, the wilderness proved less comfortable than the Egyptian provisions of their past. The crisis of freedom in the wilderness served to prove their need for God (Ex. 12-17). Israel murmured to God, unhappy with the sparse provisions (Ex. 16).

Self-government through priests and judges gave structure for civility (Ex. 18-19). God's people had to be taught what He expected of them. They must learn, follow, and be set apart to walk with their God.

God Provided Protection through Laws and Justice

The rest of Exodus is the revelation of God's laws for His people. Not only would those who follow Him flourish, but a world with morals and civility would mutually benefit. A world that can see God's blessings is a world more ready to consider a relationship with Him. God's provision of common grace was given through His lineage, just as He promised Abraham in Genesis 12.

On Mount Sinai, Moses received and gave the people God's moral, civil, and ceremonial laws. God's moral laws—the Ten Commandments—would not only strengthen Israel as they learn to be holy and recognize their sin (Rom. 3). But also the world is blessed as God's common grace falls on His creation (Ex. 20 and Appendix II, page 253).

Civil and worship laws would protect God's own people, their local relationships, and their faith (Ex. 21-27). Tribal organization provided by God gave a basis for strength through use of gifts and responsibilities (Ex. 31, 32:28). God called people *"with ability and intelligence, with knowledge and all craftsmanship,"* (Ex. 31:3).

But, how quickly the people forgot their God! Discipline was introduced in order to use the laws personally (Ex. 32). God rebuked those who didn't follow the laws because of His love for all of His creation. Sin has future consequences through generations (Ex. 34:7), passing down through nations and families. Israel was warned about dealing with other nations that worship idols (Ex. 34:12-16), which would lead to inter-marriage with sinful, idolatrous descendants.

God had laid out the pattern for the tabernacle to be built in the wilderness—a place to know and worship God. After God judged harshly the people for their worship of other gods—the golden calves—the tabernacle was constructed and dedicated (Ex. 40).

The Tabernacle was built to be the center of Israel (Ex. 36-40). *"For the cloud of the Lord was on the tabernacle by day, and fire was in it by night, in the sight of all the house of Israel throughout all their journeys,"* (Ex. 40:38).

CONSIDER how God, in an offer of covenant redemption, led His people out of sinful captivity—bondage—toward a promised place of protection, freedom, justice and prosperity. Consider how we have an even better offer as His Son Jesus Christ takes our bondage and sin away for us, leading us to the Father Creator we long to know.

SIN, SACRIFICE AND HOLINESS

LEVITICUS

In Genesis and Exodus, God created His people in His image, taught them about sin and selfishness, cursed evil when they were tempted, gave them a covenant of redemption, freed them from bondage, and gave to them laws and justice. In Leviticus we see how God, as part of this covenant redemption, sets apart His people to know and follow Him through sacrificial selflessness and a new, sanctified walk.

QUESTIONS FOR PERSONAL THOUGHT AND DISCUSSION

1. Read Lev. 1:1-4 and 7:37-38—God Taught Sacrifice as a Way to be Holy

a. What kind of offering were the Israelites to bring? (See 1:3.) What is the purpose of God accepting the offering? (See 1:4.) Define atonement.

b. What are the main types of sacrificial offerings? (See 7:37-38.) When and where did God command these offerings?

2. Read Lev. 4:1-3, 20-26, 31-35 and Heb. 7:22-28— Priests Made Atonement in Sin Offerings

a. What were priests' roles in Israel's sin offerings? (4:1-3, 20.)

b. Compare Jesus' role in being your "permanent high priest." (See Heb. 7:22-28.) When did His sacrifice occur? (See 7:27.)

3. Read Lev. 11:1-8, 44-47—God Protected Health by Designating Healthy Foods and Practices

a. How did God protect Israel in diet? (See 11:44-47.) From contagious disease? (See 13:45-46.)

b. What things do you think nomadic Israel gained from God's dietary and health restrictions? (See 11:44.)

c. How today can we be holy? What are our sacrifices? (See Rom. 12:1-2.)

4. Read Lev. 16:6-10, 30-34—Aaron Offered a Bull and Two Goats as Sacrifices and Scapegoat

a. What was the Atonement Day and what was its purpose? (See 16:30-34.)

_____

_____

b. For what purposes were the bull and first goat sacrificed? (See 16:16.)

_____

_____

c. What is the purpose of the live scapegoat? (See 16:21-22.) How is Christ our "live scapegoat"? (See Luke 24:45-48.)

_____

_____

d. How is Christ our high priest and sacrifice? (See Heb. 9:11-22.) Our eternal redeemer and mediator of a new covenant?

_____

_____

5. Read Lev. 17:1-5—Israel to Make Tent Offerings

Why do you think God made the public tent the place for sacrifice and forgiveness?

_____

6. Read Lev. 17:10-12, Heb. 13:20 and 1 John 1:7—Only Blood for Sacrifice; Life Is in the Blood

a. How was blood the symbol of Israel's sacrifice? (See 17:11.)

b. What is the eternal covenant? (See Heb. 13:20.)

c. What does it mean to "walk in the light in fellowship with Jesus"? (See 1 John 1:7.)

7. Read Lev. 25:1-12—Sabbatical and Jubilee Years

a. What explicitly did the people do in the 6 years and not do in the 7th year? What purposes do these "Sabbath rests" have?

b. What do they do and not do in the 50th year? (See 25:8-22.)

LESSON 4 SUMMARY

SIN, SACRIFICE AND HOLINESS

LEVITICUS

God Calls Us to Him in Worship and Sacrifice

In Leviticus God gave His priests and people specific ways to be holy—in God's presence and image as they were designed. God said, *"you shall therefore be holy, for I am holy,"* (Lev. 11:45).

While Leviticus is the third of the five books called the "law of Moses," or the Pentateuch, it is also a blending of two somewhat incompatible concepts—law and grace.

On the one hand, the book is one of the most legalistic works, demanding that all men render obedience to all the moral laws of God. On the other hand, it is clear that legal obedience was required only as the response to God's covenant redemption offer of mercy and grace.

CONSIDER how in Exodus God delivered His people from the slavery bondage of Egypt—from evil captivity—to a new life as a young, emerging nation of God. Consider how we each have been delivered from certain captive, binding sins to a new life of freedom in Christ. But think about how becoming holy, sanctified and Christ-like requires sacrifices and boundaries in our lives. God had a covenant plan for Israel as He does for us. We can revisit His ten commandments just as Moses urged Israel to do so. We can learn to put aside old captive habits for holy worship and sacrifice. Consider how the Levites encouraged and led God's people in worship, in holiness, and in a new, sanctified life. Consider also how God would have you learn His plan for your life—redeemed to Himself through your High Priest Jesus Christ.

Of the twelve tribes of Israel, the priests were drawn from the Levite tribe—the family of Levi. The Levites and priests instructed the people in their holiness and worship. They were the ministers of their day. They also regulated as judges the moral, civil, and ceremonial laws, and supervised the health, justice and welfare of the nation.

Sacrifices Offered for Worship and Covering of Sin

There were several kinds of sacrifice offerings recorded (Lev. 1-5; 7:37). These fulfilled two general purposes—worship and forgiveness of sin. The four worship offerings, all voluntary, were burnt (Lev. 1), grain (Lev. 2), fellowship or peace offerings (Lev. 3), and ordination (Lev. 6). They showed praise, thankfulness and devotion, resulting in access to God. Two forgiveness offerings, both required, were for sin (Lev. 4) and guilt (Lev. 5). They resulted in obedience to God.

This is called atonement—the covering and removal of guilt and sin. It made them "at one" with God. Animal offerings demonstrated that the person was giving his or her life to God by means of the life of the animal. No atonement for sin was possible without the sacrifice of life.

Guilt complexes of moral sin—personal burdens—were preventing God's people from being blessings to others, which was their covenant and reason for following God. Until their own personal burdens were lifted they couldn't minister to others' needs.

As God's covenant people, they were to be blessed to be a blessing to others, and to the world. The Levites were called by God to teach and uphold His people's understanding of sacrifice. As these sacrifices were laws, the priests acted as judges to uphold these worship laws.

Health risks as well as the need for discipline for following God's commands brought rules for foods that were allowed or forbidden. Those people who were unhealthy were diagnosed, treated, and/or separated for the health of the community (Lev. 11-13).

In the Old Testament Day of Atonement, animal sacrifice meant their sins were "covered," but not removed (Lev. 16) as Christ does in the New Testament. This "covering" of sin before Christ's death can be likened to "covering" a check written on an account in which the amount will be covered later (Heb. 9-10).

Scapegoats Took Away Confessed Sins

A scapegoat was offered to remove sins and iniquities (Lev. 16). The live goat would be freed to take away the sins of all Israel just as Christ would later rise from death taking away the sins of all believers.

Sacrifices were allowed only at the Tabernacle. God gave the people a visual safe haven for His consecration and redemption (Lev. 17).

Another preparation of God's people for receiving forgiveness in sacrifice was an understanding that *"Life is in the blood."* Blood became the symbol for life itself (Lev. 17). If Christ's life was to be God's choice of redemption for man, then His blood would forever become the symbol for the life sacrifice. God began preparing the whole world for Christ's sacrifice with this instruction and symbol.

Sanctification Provided through Conduct and Separation

God laid out rules on sexual relations (Lev. 18) with warnings, *"do not defile yourselves by any of these things"* He required in holiness and personal conduct the law of love (Lev. 19), *"You shall be holy; for I the Lord your God am holy."*

Separation for the people (Lev. 20) was for their protection and strengthening, so that they would be God's people—separated to Him. He said, *"You shall be holy to me; for I the Lord am holy, and have separated you from the peoples, that you should be mine."*

Israel Celebrated God's Provisions in Sabbatical and Jubilee Years

God provided sabbatical and jubilee periods for His people's redemption and community strengthening (Lev. 25). Relationship would be strong in God's nation and land. God wanted His people to worship Him in celebration of His granting them forgiveness, and recognizing His provision and in joy of the blessings they received and shared with others.

God, as part of His covenant redemption, led His people to know and follow Him through sacrificial selflessness and a new, sanctified walk.

CONSIDER how God constantly changes us into His holiness when we listen to Him and follow Him. Consider the covenant He promised to Abraham and Sarah, and where you may fit in the many generations of covenantal believers who were blessed to be a blessing to the world God made. Think about the moral laws that frame the most blessed nations today, and how He calls each of us to live within them, to know and remember His great justice and perfection, and to celebrate Him in our sacrifices and worship. Consider today the freedom given us by Jesus Christ who redeemed us into His mercy and grace, and the joy you have in celebrating your blessings from your Creator.

ORGANIZATION, TRIALS AND TESTING

NUMBERS

In Numbers God equips, leads, and teaches His people to trust and follow Him through trials in a new, sanctified, stronger walk—from Mt. Sinai to Canaan. Blessed to be a blessing to the world, Israel must become the holy nation that God promised it would be.

QUESTIONS FOR PERSONAL THOUGHT AND DISCUSSION

1. Read Num. 1:1-4 and 2:1-2, 17, 32-34—God Ordered a Census and Organized Camp

a. Why did God order the numbering of His people? (See also 26:1-4, 51-56.)

_____

_____

b. How was the camping to be organized by each tribe? (See 2:1-2.) What and who would be at the center? Why? (See 2:17, 32-34.)

_____

_____

c. What were roles and responsibilities of the Levites? (See 3:5-10.) What is our "priesthood" role today? (See 1 Pet. 2:5, 9.)

_____

_____

2. Read Num. 5:5-7, 6:1-5, 13-15 and 30:1-4— Confession and Vows Instituted

a. What constituted sin and confession? (See 5:5-7). What constituted restitution?

_____

b. Why do you think God instituted vows? (See 6:1-5, 13-15 and 30:1-4.) Why the specific vows for the Nazirites? (See also Judges 16:13-18.) What are some of our symbols of vows today?

_____

_____

3. Read Num. 11:1-9, 16-18— God Provided Help for His Grumbling People

a. In what physical ways does God provide for His people? (See 11:1-9 and 14:7.)

_____

b. What organization and leadership did God provide? (See 11:16-18 and 13:1-3.) What is the Spirit's role? (See 11:17.)

_____

4. Read Num. 14:1-9 and 14:20-24—God Gave Joshua and Caleb a Different Spirit

a. What did Joshua and Caleb say about the land of Canaan where God was leading them? (See 14:6-9.)

b. What was different about Caleb's spirit? (See 14:6-9, 24.)

c. What happened to the "naysayers"? (See 14:36-38.)

d. What roles did Joshua and Caleb play? (26:63-65, 27:15-20 and Josh. 1:1-3.)

5. Read Num. 20:2-12—God Said *"Tell the Rock,"* but Moses Struck the Rock Instead

a. What were Moses and the people quarreling about? (See 20:2-5.)

b. What did God ask Moses to say or do? (See 20:8-9.) How did Moses respond? (See 20:10-11.)

c. How did God respond to Moses' lack of faith? (See 20:12.) When later did Moses appear in the promised land? (See Matt. 17:1-5.)

6. Read Num. 25:1-18, 10:6-20, 11:1-9—God Exercised Vengeance through War Against Sin

a. How did God use war as an instrument of His vengeance against the sins of the Midianites? What were Israel's sins? (See 25:1-5.)

_____

_____

b. Is God just in avenging sin among His people? (See 25:8, 12-13.) Does God stage war against sin today? How?

_____

_____

7. Read Num. 33:50-56—God Promised Land Grants as Faithful Reminder of Covenant

a. What two things specifically did God want removed as they entered and received land? (See 33:52.) Why? (See 33:55.)

_____

_____

b. How does this relate to God's covenant promise to Israel? (See Gen. 17:6-8.)

_____

_____

ORGANIZATION, TRIALS AND TESTING

NUMBERS

God Organized His People

In the latter part of Exodus and throughout Numbers, we see God using trials and tests that led to Israel's organization to become a new nation. What could have been an 11-day journey for the people of Israel from Mt. Sinai to Canaan turned into a 40-year struggle. Once freed from the Egyptians, at Mt. Sinai they were equipped by God with their new laws. They were off to Canaan where they would eventually reap the promises that God made in the covenant with Abraham.

But God required their trust in Him. For Israel to reap the promises God laid out for them, they had to wander through their weaknesses before Him and be made strong by Him—not just strong enough to conquer other nations, but strong enough to trust their God fully.

CONSIDER how God allowed Israel to grow exponentially under Egypt's bondage of slavery, but recognized that they lacked the strength of a nation that leads and governs itself with freedoms and disciplines of sovereignty. Consider how the Creator God made each person in His own image—creative, wise, capable, forgiving, loving and merciful. The God of Numbers recognized that His created Israel must be organized for battle, sanctified and holy for worship, tested for strength and endurance, and blessed with God's mercy and grace in order to bless others and the world. Consider your own trials, journeys, growth and blessings through your walk following Jesus Christ.

Accountability and responsibility were both blessings and commands of God. God's "tough love" required their deliberate obedience to his laws, trust, and plan. The journey from Egypt to Canaan was more than just a trip or passage—it was a migration of an entire nation with all their possessions. The books of Exodus, Numbers and Deuteronomy all describe the struggles, defeats, and victories which this massive migration experienced as it plodded through desert and wilderness in search of its promised covenant land.

Crisis after Crisis Occurred

In these crises God taught His people trust—in Him and in His plan. He provided all they needed for their journey—both physical and spiritual. Through God's care the people became strong.

Organization developed. Rulers were appointed. A census—numbering of God's people—is recorded in Numbers 1:18-19, they *"registered themselves by clans, by fathers' houses, according to the number of names from twenty years old and upward, head by head, as the Lord commanded Moses. So he listed them in the wilderness of Sinai."*

Camping Details Given to Tribes and Families

Each tribe was instructed how and where to prepare their camp, and each camp faced the Tabernacle meeting tent for worship (Num.2). Discipline was required for trusting God. To receive God's covenant promise and fulfill its blessing to *"be a blessing to the whole world,"* (Gen. 12) discipline was essential to trust God and use His laws, means of worship, and protection. The Levites were prominent with their instructions to serve as priests, justices and worship leaders at the center of the community (Num. 3).

Confessions and Vows of Discipline Were Instituted, Committing Themselves to God

God ordered confessions of sin and restitution for wrongs committed against others when a person realized his guilt (Num. 5). Vows of discipline and commitment were instituted (Num. 6). Orderly movement of the tribes were developed. Breaking camp was carefully planned with the tabernacle and the Ark of the Covenant (Num. 10).

God Filled Needs through Trials

Physical discomforts that followed their exodus from Egypt led them to desperation (Num. 11-20). God responded by filling all their needs. He quenched hunger with manna and quail, thirst with water, and gave leadership with priests and elders. The hardships toward freedom's blessings required total trust in their leader Moses and Provider God.

The people's physical wanting led to accusations (Num. 14:2): *"And all the people of Israel grumbled against Moses and Aaron. The whole congregation said to them, "Would that we had died in the land of Egypt! Or would that we had died in this wilderness!"* Moses and Aaron went to the Lord, who promised the people water if Moses simply asked the rock to produce it. Instead, Moses struck the rock with his staff and was denied entrance into the promised Canaan with his people (Num. 20).

Israel Set Out for Red Sea toward Canaan

They set out to the Red Sea, to go around the land of Edom, and became impatient (Num. 21). *"And the people spoke against God and against Moses, 'Why have you brought us up out of Egypt to die in the wilderness? For there is no food and no water, and we loathe this worthless food,'"* (Num. 21:5). God struck the grumbling people with fiery serpents and many died. Following confessions of their sin God instructed Moses to *"Make a fiery serpent and set it on a pole, and everyone who is bitten, when he sees it, shall live,"* (Num. 21:8). The serpent-pole is an image of Christ's crucifixion offering salvation to those in need of mercy and grace (John 3:14).

God took vengeance in His war against sin. After Israel began to mix with *"the daughters of Moab,"* and bowed down to their Baal gods. *"the Lord spoke to Moses, saying, 'Harass the Midianites and strike them down, for they have harassed you,'"* (Num. 25).

God was just to those who did and didn't trust Him. The sons of Reuben and Gad didn't want to cross the Jordan for the land that was promised them. God said, after blessing Caleb and Joshua for fully trusting Him, that none of the others would see the land (Num. 32). He accomplished this by making them *"wander in the wilderness for forty years until all the generation that had done evil...was consumed."*

God accomplished His provision for Israel, as well as His vengeance against sin through His justice over evil in Canaan.

God's promises to His people never changed—from Abraham, to Moses, to Joshua, to you and me. God equipped, led, and taught His people to trust and follow Him in a new, sanctified walk. His words to Moses are for us today—Num. 6:22-27 records, *"The Lord spoke to Moses, saying, 'Speak to Aaron and his sons, saying, Thus you shall bless the people of Israel: you shall say to them, The Lord bless you and keep you; the Lord make his face to shine upon you and be gracious to you; the Lord lift up his countenance upon you and give you peace.' So shall they put my name upon the people of Israel, and I will bless them.'"*

CONSIDER how our grumbling and complaining must sound to our Provider-Creator God! Think about the steps God went through with His covenant Israel before they were the strong, holy people He made them to become. Consider how God has plans for your future for which He is equipping, testing, leading and preparing you. Can you count your blessings in worship and praise for your Provider Jesus Christ who leads you through this life giving your promised blessings to your world?

DISCIPLINE AND OBEDIENCE

DEUTERONOMY

Exodus, Leviticus and Numbers together narrate Israel's 40 years of wandering and distrust of God's plan and provisions, after God sent His people to complete their covenant mission—to be a blessing for the world. In Deuteronomy—which means "second telling of the law"—Moses reviewed in three sermons God's plan for His people and gave guidance, passionately reminding them of their covenant mission.

QUESTIONS FOR PERSONAL THOUGHT AND DISCUSSION

1. Read Deut. 1:1-8 and Num. 33:50-56—Moses Reminded Israel of God's Laws and Plan

a. How long had they traveled compared to the actual distance? (See 1:2-3.) What instructions did Moses give on November 1 of the 40th year after the Exodus? Where were they to go and why? (See 1:6-8 and Num. 33:50-56.)

b. How had Israel grown since going into Egypt as 70 people of Jacob's family? (See Deut. 1:8-11 and Gen. 15:5-6.)

2. Read Deut. 3:18-22—God Provided a Military Plan and Family Protections

a. Describe God's plan for military "valor" and troops to claim the promised land. (See 3:18.)

b. How did God's plan protect the families and possessions? (See 3:19-20.)

3. Read Deut. 4:1-14 and 11:18-25—Israel Forgot and Ignored its Laws and Statutes

a. How many of the laws were the people to know and obey? (See 4:1-2.) Compare 4:2 with Rev. 22:18-19.

b. What benefits would the laws and statutes give Israel? (See 4:6-8.)

c. How would future generations teach and receive the laws? (See 4:9-14, 6:6-9 and 11:18-25.)

4. Read Deut. 4:15-19—God Commanded Against Idols, Nature Worship and Astrology

Describe the kinds of idolatry with which the world and Satan might tempt God's people.

_____

_____

5. Read Deut. 9:1-6—God Drove out Wickedness in His War Against Sin and Evil

Why did God's covenant plan need to remove the native inhabitants of Canaan? What is the moral warning God gave His people and why? (See 9:4-6.)

_____

_____

6. Read Deut. 14:22-29—God's People were Taught to Tithe Offerings to Their Provider

a. Who chose the place God's people would tithe? (See 14:23.)

_____

b. For what four reasons connected to God were they to tithe? (See 14:23, 29.) How might these apply today?

_____

_____

7. Read Deut. 24:1-5—God Gave Laws for Marriage and Honeymoons

How do you think healthy marriages strengthened Israel's communities, families and nation? Why were the certificates and reasons necessary?

_____

_____

8. Read Deut. 28:1-24—God Distinguished Obedience from Disobedience

a. What were God's blessings of obedience? (See 28:1-14.)

_____

_____

b. What were some of God's curses of disobedience? (See 28:15-24.)

_____

_____

9. Read Deut. 30:15-20 and 32:44-47—Moses Urged the People to "Choose Life"

How do we choose life and good over death and evil? What were Moses' final words to Israel?

_____

_____

LESSON 6 SUMMARY

DISCIPLINE AND OBEDIENCE
DEUTERONOMY

Moses Urged God's People to Follow Him

Deuteronomy is Moses' final plea for his people to utilize fully the provisions God had given them. Not just food for the day, but an organized military nation ready to possess what God had promised them. Moses' discourses aren't only important because he was old and dying, or because the people hadn't entered Canaan. More importantly the people were a new generation who had heard God's plan through the laws, but hadn't begun to live it daily or pass it along to their future generations.

In this book God lovingly reminds His people of his covenants, laws and statutes, equipping and empowering them for their promised relationship with their God and Creator.

How quickly God's people had forgotten their blessings and responsibilities! God had promised His people a future of strength and blessings so great that they, in turn, would bless the whole world.

CONSIDER how patient and trusting God was with Moses and His people. As sin and evil encroached on every side, God gave Moses the words to faithfully remind and prepare the people to follow the laws, and to honor, worship, and follow God in the blessings He promised.

Consider how quickly we, too, forget God's laws and plans for our lives. We might look to Moses' words here to remind ourselves how He provides more than we ever asked, that we might fully trust and follow Him in Christ Jesus. We too are part of the covenant blessing to the world around us!

God had provided for their basic needs, and promised complete abundance. All His people needed was to trust and follow their God. God had commissioned Moses the leader to prepare the people of Israel to be the nation of Israel—and the nation of God. Moses reminded them what they needed to achieve God's plan—not their own plan.

Moses Reiterated God's Faithfulness

Moses' passionate pleas came in the form of three speeches, sometimes called sermons, to the people on the plains of Moab. The first speech was the reminder of God's plan and recent provisions (Deut. 1-4:43). Moses recalled the recent past to re-establish order by reminding the people of God's faithful judgment on Israel's unbelief and the deliverance and provision when they believe.

God, through Moses, retraced for His people how he guided them to Moab and provided leaders (Deut. 1), provided victories over the Amorites (Deut. 2), and appointed Joshua to lead them to Canaan (Deut. 3). God gave the people military guidance for war and family provisions for safety with specific promises (Deut. 3).

God reminded His people of their righteous core rules and statutes—not to add nor take away from them—which would make Israel great with a God nearby. As idolatry and nature worship spread, Israel was warned not to engage in their sinful evil (Deut. 4).

Moses said, *"For what great nation is there that has a god so near to it as the Lord our God is to us, whenever we call upon him? And what great nation is there, that has statutes and rules so righteous as all this law that I set before you today?"* (Deut. 4:7-8).

Moses Repeated the Laws and Statutes

The second speech began with a reiteration of the laws and statutes (Deut. 4:44-5). This sermon is long and thorough because the nation's future depended fully on its discipline for obedience in relationship with God. Three sections of the speech are: testimonies of moral duties expanding the Ten Commandments, and duties for using and teaching them (Deut. 5-11); statutes of ceremonial duties including sacrifices, tithes and feasts (Deut. 12-16); and ordinances of civil and social duties, including justice, criminal law, warfare rules, property, personal and family morality, and social justice (Deut. 16-26).

Moses repeated the Ten Commandments and emphasized that they are a covenant with God (Deut. 5). He told them of the law of love, which became their Hebrew Creed (Deut. 6). Moses emphasized that God is not to be tested in keeping His laws. Moses connected mankind to God in saying, *"man does not live by bread alone,"* and *"as a man disciplines his son, the Lord your God disciplines you,"* (Deut. 8). Moses warned, *"It is not by our righteousness but others' wickedness"* that God confirms to us His promises (Deut. 9). God established the law of the tithe as a financial sacrifice (Deut. 14). He gave marriage laws of divorce, honeymoon, etc., along with the other civil laws, to keep His people civilly strong (Deut. 24).

Moses Ratified the Covenant and Requirements for Discipline and Obedience

The third and final talk was a ratification of the covenant with Israel (Deut. 27-34). Moses gave his prophecy of Israel's future. He clearly distinguished obedience and disobedience, along with God's response to each (Deut. 28). With obedience comes blessings but with disobedience comes punishment. Moses reminded the people of God's covenant and its terms. He called on them to *"choose life,"* (Deut. 30) and said, *"it is not a trivial thing,"* (Deut. 32).

He said, *"I have set before you life and death, blessing and curse. Therefore choose life, that you and your offspring may live, loving the Lord your God, obeying his voice and holding fast to him, for he is your life and length of days, that you may dwell in the land that the Lord swore to your fathers, to Abraham, to Isaac, and to Jacob, to give them,"* (Deut. 30:19-20).

Moses finished writing the Pentateuch by completing the reiterated laws in this book and commanded the Levites to, *"Take this Book of the Law and put it by the side of the ark of the covenant of the Lord your God, that it may be there for a witness against you,"* (Deut. 31: 26). Then Moses led his "Song of Moses" for the people to recite over generations (Deut. 31).

As Moses concluded his final talk, he said, *"Take to heart all the words by which I am warning you today, that you may command them to your children, that they may be careful to do all the words of this law. For it is no empty word for you, but your very life, and by this word you shall live long in the land that you are going over the Jordan to possess,"* (Deut. 32:46-47).

He appointed Joshua his successor before giving his final address with plea for choosing God. God called him up to Mount Nebo, which is opposite Jericho. *"And the Lord said to him, 'This is the land of which I swore to Abraham, to Isaac, and to Jacob, I will give it to your offspring. I have let you see it with your eyes, but you shall not go over there.' So Moses the servant of the Lord died there in the land of Moab, according to the word of the Lord,"* (Deut. 34:4-5).

CONSIDER how God, through Moses in Deuteronomy, lovingly reminded His people of His covenants, laws and statutes, equipping and empowering them for their destined relationship with their God and Creator. Consider today reminding yourself of the journey on which God is leading you. Think of the blessings of life you have received, the trials from which you have been rescued, and the joyful opportunities Christ gives you to share His blessings with others in this fallen world.

CONQUERING AND CONQUESTS

JOSHUA

In the book of Joshua God leads His people into Canaan—personally and collectively—in a war against sin. Together, they are striving toward the covenant plan of being blessed by God and becoming a blessing for the whole world.

QUESTIONS FOR PERSONAL THOUGHT AND DISCUSSION

1. Read Josh. 1:1-9 and Gen. 12:1-4—Joshua Assumed Leadership for the Covenant Passage

a. How does God's call of Joshua to lead His people compare to that of Abraham?

b. Compare Abraham's response (Gen. 12:4), Joshua's response (Josh. 1:10-11), and Israel's response (1:16-18).

c. Compare also Moses' call (Ex. 3:4-10) and responses (Ex. 3:11, 13, 4:1, 10 and 13.) Consider also Deut. 34:4.

2. Read Josh. 2:1-14—God Used Rahab's Position and Testimony to Take Jericho

a. Describe Rahab's occupation, reputation and connection to the king. (See 2:1-3.)

_____

_____

b. Describe Rahab's belief and faith in Israel's God. (See 2:8-13 and 6:15-17, 22-25.) Describe her salvation. (See also Matt. 1:5.)

_____

_____

c. Do you think Rahab's falsehoods and cover ups were sins or faithfulness? (See 2:3-7.) Why? How did God use her?

_____

3. Read Josh. 3:5-11 and 4:4-7—The Ark of the Covenant and Memorial Stones Were Symbols

a. How did God use the Ark of the Covenant and Moses' Laws to strengthen and remind His people through this Jordan River passage? (See 3:3-11, 16-17.)

_____

b. How were the Memorial Stones used for signs of each tribe? For teaching future generations? How do the Red Sea and Jordan River crossings compare? (See 4:19-24.)

_____

4. Read Josh. 5:1, 13-15—God Melted Spirits of Local Kings, and Commander of Army Appears

a. How did God prepare for Israel to take control of the Promised Land?

b. Were the people prepared to win control on their own? (See also Deut. 3:18-22.)

c. Who do you think is the "Commander of the Lord's Army"? Compare with Ex. 3:5.

5. Read Josh. 6:18-19 and 8:20-22—Faith was Broken and Israel Defeated at Ai

a. What was God's instruction for the spoils of Jericho? (See 6:18-19, 24.)

b. What did Achan do, and what was God's reaction? (See 7:1, 10-13.) Read Joshua's reaction and Achan's confession. (See 7:19-21.)

c. Do you think God hates sinful people or sin itself? In Jericho and Ai, was God at war with people or at war against sin?

6. Read Josh. 8:24-28, and 12:7-24—Israel Defeated Ai, All of South and North Canaan

a. Read also 8:30-35. How did Joshua strengthen God's people for the war against sinful Canaan?

b. Read also 11:6-8. How did God counsel Joshua and weaken Israel's enemies?

7. Read Josh. 13:1-7, Scan 13:8-22:34—Joshua Allotted Land; Philistines Remained a Threat

a. How did the allotment of land fulfill God's covenant with Abraham? (Compare Josh. 1:1-11 with Gen. 12:1-4.)

b. In what way were the Philistine and Gaza areas still a threat? (See 13:1-7, Judges 3:1-6 and 1 Sam. 4:1-11.)

c. Read Joshua's farewell in 24:14-15. What were his fears for the peoples' faith? What is their response (See 24:16-19.)

d. Read 24:19. How today does Jesus make us able to serve a Holy God and bring us forgiveness of transgressions?

CONQUERING AND CONQUESTS

JOSHUA

Joshua Led the Conquests for Canaan

In the conquest for Canaan the people feared their foes, but Joshua led them anyway in God's protection and to His provisions. While God provided settlement of the Holy Land, the conquest was still incomplete (Josh. 1-12). As they settled, God, through Joshua, allotted land and provisions (Josh. 13-21). God's conditions for the blessings were simply choosing to serve their God (Josh. 22-24).

God's deliverance to Canaan illustrates His faithfulness, His vengeance against personal sin, and His vengeance against corporate and national sin. He uses anyone and anything to deliver His people from sin. But He requires their heartfelt faithfulness. Joshua's experience entering Canaan illustrates God's vengeance against sin, and His deliverance from it in a covenant of grace and faith.

CONSIDER how God is a God of war—against sin. He wants us to conquer sin in our own lives first, and in our world, second, in order to be a blessing for all of His creation. So, God does use war—against sin. The story of Joshua and Israel's conquest is a story of God's deliverance of His people from wandering and confusion, in a faithless state, to victory over sin in a faithful state.

Consider how you can be victorious over sin in your own life and world by trusting God and Jesus Christ to redeem and fully sanctify you and those around you.

In the conquest of Canaan (Josh. 1-12), Israel moved forward in four stages: they mobilized, advanced, attacked, and reflected in an evaluation of God's conquest of this rich but sinful land. The call to arms began with God's call to Joshua. His right of entrance to the land was that God had given it to him and His people. Their power to enter was from God. And their success depended that Joshua and troops would be strong, courageous and obedient to God's laws.

Joshua Was Commissioned and Called the People

In Joshua 1:5-6 God said, *"No man shall be able to stand before you all the days of your life. Just as I was with Moses, so I will be with you. I will not leave you or forsake you. Be strong and courageous, for you shall cause this people to inherit the land that I swore to their fathers to give them."*

Urgently within three days they were to move forward. Almost 40 years before the spies had been sent, and Joshua and Caleb brought back the true, faithful report. Joshua now sent spies again, but this time they had faith that God would direct and protect them.

God Used Rahab and Her Faith to Take Jericho

When the spies met Rahab they realized God's presence and control. Rahab said to them, *"I know that the Lord has given you the land, and that the fear of you has fallen upon us, and that all the inhabitants of the land melt away before you. For we have heard how the Lord dried up the water of the Red Sea before you when you came out of Egypt, and what you did to the two kings of the Amorites who were beyond the Jordan, to Sihon and Og, whom you devoted to destruction. And as soon as we heard it, our hearts melted, and there was no spirit left in any man because of you, for the Lord your God, he is God in the heavens above and on the earth beneath,"* (Josh. 2:9-11).

Rahab asked for their protection. The spies came back with their report that God's promise was being fulfilled. According to Rahab, *"their terror was fallen upon the people."* Rahab instilled faith in the Israelites because of God's faithfulness and her witness.

Israel Crossed the Jordan to the Promised Canaan

The first movement of the people of Israel in their crossing of the Jordan River displayed their right relationship with God (Josh. 3). Joshua 3:17 reads, *"Now the priests bearing the ark of the covenant of the Lord stood firmly on dry ground in the midst of the Jordan, and all Israel was passing over on dry ground until all the nation finished passing over the Jordan."*

They entered Canaan not by bridging the river or by deflecting the water, but by God's divine intervention. While the mission demanded their haste, the people were not allowed to forget or neglect worship and their thanksgiving to God afterward (Josh. 4).

Ark of the Covenant and Memorial Stones Became Permanent Worship Symbols

The ceremony of stones was observed when they were safely over the river. The miraculous crossing of the river had a remarkable effect on the surrounding people, *"their heart melted, neither was there any spirit in them anymore."*

Then God led Joshua to recognize his authority and leadership depended on his submission and obedience through worship and re-circumcision (Josh. 5). After this submission, God granted them sustenance of the new land, and declared *"This land is holy."*

With the preparation, the people of Israel became the scourge of God, moving forward in His judgment upon the corrupt peoples of the land. Jericho was overtaken in fear and Rahab protected in faith (Josh. 6).

Their victory was obviously in their weakness and total dependency on God. Marching priests and blasting horns are useless in warfare. The victory was theirs, but they were taught that it was not by their might, but by their obedience to the government of their Holy God.

Faith was Broken and Israel Defeated at Ai

Then, suddenly their triumphant might was defeated in Ai, when Achan broke the faith (Josh. 7). The sin of one man felled the entire army. After dealing with Achan's sin, the new army conquered Ai and they thanked God in worship and teaching (Josh. 8).

Word spread quickly. The fame of this successful, God-driven nation spread, and kings of the surrounding peoples formed a league against Canaan. All kings united against Israel, except the Gibeonites with their plot to be Israel's servants (Josh. 9).

The strategy of the Gibeonites threatened Israel, but Joshua took immediate and decisive action. Modern Canaan was in awe, as the Gibeonites had been a powerful and respected nation. Israel persisted in battle, and all the lands South and North were conquered (Josh. 10). Joshua 10:42 says, *"And Joshua captured all these kings and their land at one time, because the Lord God of Israel fought for Israel."*

Then the land had rest from war. In all 31 kings and their nations had been conquered, except Philistia (Josh. 12). But without the defeat of the Philistines the conquest of Canaan was not complete (Josh. 13).

Finally God's people would settle their holy, prosperous land (Josh. 13-19). Providing for His people a new justice system to uphold the laws with grace, God demonstrated that the journey was over for now. This was where His people would live. Their lives would be in civilized relationship with God providing laws and order (Josh. 20).

Lastly, before his death, Joshua demanded that the people *"Choose this day whom you will serve,"* (Josh. 24:15).

CONSIDER how God, with Joshua, led His people personally and collectively in a war against sin, striving toward the covenant plan of blessing the whole world. Consider how today we too must battle sin and evil, but how Christ our Redeemer takes on Satan and his armies in our stead. Praise God for our Savior and Redeemer!

JUSTICE AND DELIVERANCE

JUDGES AND RUTH

The book of Judges is a rotation of leaders called "judges" who deliver a falling Israel from sinful oppression and their own sinful hearts. God raised judges over all Israel calling them to return to His holy nation of worship, where they could accept priestly, sacrificial forgiveness. (See Appendix III, page 254.) God judged His people based upon whom they chose to serve. As it is now, when His people sought and served Him, God delivered them from evil.

QUESTIONS FOR PERSONAL THOUGHT AND DISCUSSION

1. Read Jud. 1:27-32 and 2:1-4, 11-15—Israel Disobeyed God, Mixing with Sinful Nations

a. How did Canaan's locals become threats to Israel? (See 1:27-32 and 3:1-6.)

b. What are five consecutive things the people did in a downward spiral? (See 2:11-12.)

c. What was God's response in 2:14? Was this fair? Describe God's justice, mercy and grace. (See 2:16-18.)

2. Scan Jud. 3:7-31—God Raised Up Othniel, Ehud and Shamgar as His Judges

a. Who was Othniel and what was his relationship with God? (See 3:9-11.) How many years did Othniel serve as judge, and how did Israel respond? Why? (See 3:10-11.)

b. Who was Ehud and what was his relationship with God? (See 3:15, 28-30.) How did Ehud bring God's judgment on the enemies? How many years did Ehud judge?

d. Who was Shamgar and what did he accomplish? (See 3:31.)

3. Read Jud. 4:1-8—God Called Deborah and Barak

a. What was the state of Israel under King Jabin of Canaan? What was Deborah's occupation when God called her?

b. What roles did Deborah and Barak take on in serving God? (See 4:6-10.) What was the outcome? (See 4:15-16, 23-24.)

4. Scan Jud. 6-8—Gideon Defeated the Midianites

a. What were causes and results of Israel's broken relationship with God? (See 6:1-6.)

b. Compare the prophet God sent to Israel (6:7-10) with the angel God sent to Gideon (6:11-18). What was the angel's true identity, and Gideon's reaction? (See 6:19-24.)

c. Why did Gideon take only 300 men to defeat the Midianites rather than 32,000? (See 7:1-3, 15-25.)

d. What was their reaction after the defeat, and Gideon's response? (See 8:22-23.) What happened after Gideon died? (See 8:33-35.)

5. Read Jud. 9:1-6, 22-25—The People Debated God's Rule Versus a King's Rule

a. Compare 8:22-23 with 9:1-6? How did Abimelech conspire to become a king like other nations have?

b. Was Israel seeking God's holy laws or a king's human might?

6. Read Jud. 11:1-15 and 12:7-13:7—God Called Jephthah and Samson to Rescue Israel

a. What were Jephthah's background and qualifications to rule over Israel? (See 11:7-15.)

b. What was the state of Israel when Samson was born? (See 13:1.) Why do you think God picked these Nazirites to bear Samson? (See 13:21-25.)

c. After a colorful life, God allowed Samson to bring down the Philistines. (See 16:28-31.) Describe his faith in God.

d. After Samson's death, no judges upheld God's laws. (See 21:25.) Who did the people follow without God's judges?

7. Read Ruth 1:1-6 and 2:1-4—Ruth and Naomi

a. Who were the three widows and why were they in the fields? (See 1:1-6.) Describe the faith of Ruth. (See 1:15-18.)

b. How did God lead and bless these women? How did Boaz greet them? (See 1:22-2:4.)

c. Connect Ruth's roles in 4:11-21 and Matt.1:5-6, 17.

LESSON 8 SUMMARY

JUSTICE AND DELIVERANCE

JUDGES AND RUTH

God Called Judges to Rescue Israel to His Laws

God introduced "judging" in Genesis where He alone is the theocratic Judge of Adam and Eve. From that day God has dealt directly with sin and evil in our lives. Human judges who were called to leadership by God began in Exodus and Leviticus when God gave the authority of judging to priests as part of worship and sacrifice to God. In Exodus and Deuteronomy, God, through Moses, gave the role of judging moral and civil cases to local judges (Ex. 18). In Judges we see God call judges (see Appendix III, page 254) during a period of a downward spiral from the "theocratic" government of God under His holy laws to the "democratic" government of man in human self-reliance. The book of Ruth is a vignette illustrating God's faithfulness and grace during this period of moral and civil disobedience.

CONSIDER how God's judgment of Israel by His appointed judges assumed innocence—unless proven guilty by moral or civil rule under God's holy laws. This is as we know justice today in our legal courts: "innocent until proven guilty." Consider how mankind in our fallen world—all of us—are unable to fully keep God's laws. We are "guilty until proven innocent" by our High Priest Jesus

Christ when we are redeemed, forgiven, and sanctified in God's justice of mercy and grace!

The book of Judges is a rotation of leaders called judges who deliver a falling Israel from sinful oppression. God raised judges over this sinful nation giving His people a chance to return to His government of worship, where they could accept priestly, sacrificial forgiveness.

Israel Periodically Cried Out to God for Salvation

After the battles of Joshua and the conquest of Canaan pagan peoples still lived among the tribes. Within a few years and generations Israel was trying to mix darkness with light (Jud. 2:11-12). God judged His people's sin by no longer protecting them from harm.

The nations of Egypt, Philistia, Assyria, and others longed to reclaim the land and power for themselves. Morally and spiritually weak, Israel became an easy prey of the Mesopotamians, Moabites, Canaanites, Midianites, Ammonites, and Philistines, each in succession. They conquered God's people into oppressive submission.

A loose confederation of tribes, weakened by years of peaceful passivity, each of Israel's tribes was vulnerable to attack. Judah— Israel's Southern territory—fought just to maintain its own land. The conquest was not complete, as locals became a threat as previously warned (Jud. 2).

Only in anguish would Israel turn back to God and call for deliverance. God gave these weak tribes strong, godly judges to be their leaders and to restore His justice and mercy under His laws.

The Bible names 13 judges in this book. They are Othniel, Ehud, Shamgar, Deborah, Barak, Gideon, Tola, Jair, Jephthah, Ibzan, Elon, Abdon, and Samson. Only six, however, are given prominent mention, and each dealt with a different sinful enemy: Othniel defeated the Mesopotamians; Ehud, the Moabites; Deborah, the Canaanites; Gideon, the Midianites; Jephthah, the Ammonites; and Samson the Philistines. In 1 Samuel, following these judges, both Eli and Samuel are also judges serving God.

Othniel became the first Judge-deliverer, and Ehud the second (Jud. 3). Othniel was Caleb's nephew. Both the uncle and nephew were characterized by their spiritual discernment and Godly leadership.

Deborah and Barak Were Called to Lead as Team

With the alliance of judge Barak, prophetess Deborah led Israel from oppression. Then she praised God in song (Jud. 5). After 40 years of peace, once again Israel turned away from the Lord, giving in to the victory and oppression of the Midianites. Life was so hard in the face of evil that the people hid themselves in dens, caves and strongholds. At last, after seven years, God answered their cries with Gideon.

Gideon Was God's Judge and Deliverer

Gideon had long contemplated the sin of the people and their broken relationship with God. Called to act as their judge and deliverer, he broke down their altars to Baal, and restored their worship to God. God told him, *"I will be with you."* Gideon, with only 300 faithful in his army, saw God's miracle as the enemy killed each other in the darkness of the night, as *"the Spirit of the Lord had come upon Gideon."*

Gideon was so strong a leader through the deliverance, the people wanted to make him king like other nations. As God's anointed judge, he refused. Gideon declared *"The Lord will rule over you—not a judge or a king,"* (Jud. 8). There was an anti-king debate over his son Abimelech, who briefly was made king of Shechem (Jud. 9). Abimelech killed his 70 brothers in defense of his title, as they were sons of Gideon.

Samson Used Nazirite Vows in Striking Philistines

Then God called Samson even before his Nazirite birth to deliver Israel from the Philistines (Jud. 13:5). God used Samson's Nazirite vows to prove his strength and that of Israel's God. He was stronger than a lion, and broke open metal chains in a show of God's strength. He gave his own life—in a sacrificial act like Christ—in knocking down an evil pagan temple with *"all the lords"* including 3,000 Philistines.

Ruth Follows Naomi and Her God in Link to Christ

Following Judges in the book of Ruth is another contrasting picture that is an appendage to the oppressive stories of Israel's failures. During the same period of Judges, in a sharp contrast to the national sin and cycles of corruption of Israel, Ruth is a story of faithfulness amid infidelity. It is also a link in the history of man to our Savior, Jesus Christ (Matt. 1).

During a famine, Ruth's family maintained their faith in God. Certainly her mother-in-law Naomi, in all her suffering, was loyal to God and her family. She unselfishly encouraged her two daughters-in-law to leave her and return to prosperity in Moab. In a choice of faith, Ruth refused to leave Naomi behind. Naomi showed her faithful devotion not only to Ruth, but to Ruth's God saying, *"Thy God my God."*

The two happened upon the portion of the field belonging to Boaz. Boaz was a godly farmer who greeted his workers, *"The Lord be with you,"* (Ruth 2). Their response was *"The Lord bless you."* Boaz, whether on his own, or responding to Naomi's encouragement, became in love with Ruth and took her for his wife (Ruth 4). Naomi was cared for in this joyful marriage. Obed, their son later became the father of Jesse, the father of David, in the lineage of Jesus Christ.

CONSIDER how God yearns for His people to serve and worship only Him. He blesses those servants to be a blessing to all His creation. Consider how, even in cycles of sin and evil, God raises up faithful servants to further His plan of covenant redemption for a fallen creation. Will we follow our Holy God even amid nations like the Philistines? Can we be more like Deborah, Ruth and Naomi—faithful believers following God and bringing peace wherever He leads us?

GOVERNMENTS OF GOD AND MAN

1, 2 SAMUEL, 1 CHRONICLES

The two books of Samuel and 1 Chronicles cover a period of great transition in the history of the nation of Israel. It is from the "theocratic" judges of God, such as Samson, Eli and Samuel, to the "autocratic" kings of men, like Saul and his many successors. (See Appendices III and IV, pages 254-255.) It is in these peoples' transition away from God that we see His plans for their self-government and for those leaders whom He calls for them.

QUESTIONS FOR PERSONAL THOUGHT AND DISCUSSION

1. Read 1 Sam. 1:1-20—Hannah Was Blessed with Son Samuel to Succeed Judge Eli

a. How did God use Hannah's emptiness to birth a devoted leader of God? (See 1:9-11.) What was Hannah's response? (See 1:21-28.) Scan her prayer in 2:1-11.

b. Since Eli was a judge over Israel, what were the prospects of his sons succeeding him as judges? (See 2:12-17, 22-25.)

c. Who called Samuel to succeed Eli, and what was Eli's response? (See 3:9-21.)

2. Read 1 Sam. 4:1-11—The Ark of the Covenant Became Israel's Coveted Idol

a. In what way(s) did the Ark of the Covenant become Israel's idol? (See 4:3-11.) Who guarded the Ark? (See 4:4.)

_____

b. What happened to Judge Eli? (See 4:15-18.) What happened to the Philistines in Ashdod, Gath and Ekron? (See 5:6-12.) Describe the idolatry and repentance when the Ark was returned. (See 6:13-21.)

_____

_____

3. Read 1 Sam. 7:1-4, 12-17, 8:1-9—Samuel and Sons Judged Israel; But Israel Cried for a King

a. How did Judge Samuel address Israel? (See 7:1-4.) How did Samuel's sons judge Israel? (See 8:3.)

_____

b. For what did the elders ask Samuel? (See 8:4-5.) What was Samuel's reaction? (See 8:6.) And God's? (See 8:9, 19-22.)

_____

4. Read 1 Sam. 9:15-17, 10:9-27—Saul Became the First King of Israel

a. What roles did the people, God, Samuel and Saul have in appointing the first King? (See 9:15-19 and 10:22-27.)

_____

b. What warnings about a king did God give the people through Samuel? (See 8:10-18 and 10:17-18.)

_____

_____

c. Read 12:11-25. Summarize Samuel's farewell address and advice for the new monarchy.

_____

d. Read the summary of Saul's reign in 14:47-52. Then read God's summary in 15:10-11 and 22-23. Compare and contrast sacrifice and obedience.

_____

5. Read 1 Sam. 16:1, 10-14 and 2 Sam. 5:1-5— Young David Anointed the Next King for Israel

a. Describe Samuel's role in the transition. (See 1 Sam. 16:1, 10-14.) Why do you think God used Samuel for the transition?

_____

b. Why was Israel divided? (See 2 Sam. 3:1.) How old was David when he was made king? How long did he reign over united Israel and Judah? (See 2 Sam. 5:1-5.)

_____

6. Read 1 Chron. 10:1-14 and 17:16-27—Saul Died, David became King and Prayed for Israel

a. Summarize Saul's reign. (See 10:13-14.) Why was David anointed king by God?

_____

b. How would you describe David's heart for God? (See 17:16-27.)

_____

c. Describe David's monarchy. (See 18:14-17 and 2 Sam. 8:15-18.)

_____

_____

7. Read 2 Sam. 5:1-10 and 1 Chron. 15:1-5—David United Israel at Jerusalem; Sinned Against God

a. Describe God's plan for David to unite Israel and Judah at Jerusalem. (See 2 Sam. 5:1-5, 9-10.)

_____

b. Describe God's plan for the Ark and the Temple, as the Prophet Nathan conveyed. (See 1 Chron. 15:1-15.)

_____

c. Describe David's sin in the Prophet Nathan's rebuke. (See 2 Sam. 12:7-9, 13.)

_____

8. 1 Chron. 28:1-8, 20-21—David Pledged to Build the Temple, Charged Role to King Solomon

Why did God assign Solomon to build the Temple. (See 28:1-10.) What condition did God place on building the Temple? (See 28:7-10.) What relationship did God require of him?

_____

_____

LESSON 9 SUMMARY

GOVERNMENTS OF GOD AND MAN

1, 2 SAMUEL, 1 CHRONICLES

Israel Rejected God's Justice for King's Strength

God's government had gone from a pure theocracy with Adam and Eve, Cain and Abel; to a priest-theocracy with Moses and the Levites; to a priest-judge leadership with Moses, Jethro, and Deborah; to a civil and military judgeship—without God at the center—in Judges.

The people's trust was turning slowly away from God. The transition of Israel in Samuel was not just a switch from judges to kings, but more importantly a change from God's direct leadership through chosen leaders of His laws to that of ever-more-secular kings.

The two books of Samuel (originally one book) and 1 Chronicles cover this period of transition in the history of the nation of Israel. That transition is of government—as we saw in Judges—is from following God's judges through worship, His laws, reconciliation and justice—to following the desires of man's personal independence to allow *"that each person did what was right in his own eyes."*

CONSIDER how Israel rejected God as their King. They left behind the theocracy of God's judges and laws, and cried out for an earthly king like those of the Philistines and other "successful" nations. And for what people ask of God, they must realize they might receive along with the consequences that follow. Consider how God desires that His leaders would bring His people into stronger relationship with God Himself, because He yearns for each of us to know Him fully and eternally. Consider how you might look to leaders who will encourage you to better know God, His Word, and your eternal Redeemer!

Israel Wanted to Self-Govern Like Other Nations

The history of these books traces the last of the judges, Eli and Samuel, through the troublesome times of their new King Saul. The people of Israel learned how difficult government by man really is.

First Samuel covers David's youth, the future king who was chosen and anointed by God. Second Samuel deals almost exclusively with the history of King David's reign. First Chronicles parallels these stories and records them for Temple history.

God Blessed Hannah with Samuel to be Last Judge

In First Samuel God answered prayers of a faithful woman. Hannah trusted God with her request, and God gave her a son to be the last judge of Israel (1 Sam. 1). This trust would offer Israel a godly leader in Samuel. While young Samuel *"grew in the fear of God"* in the Tabernacle, life outside was increasingly corrupt with human pride. Samuel was distinctly called by God when still a young boy, and trained before he assumed leadership as God's final judge over Israel (1 Sam. 3). (See Appendices III and IV, 254-255.)

Ark of the Covenant Became Philistines' Idol

Samuel foretold the crisis with the coming Philistine attack. Hoping to save themselves, Israel carried the Ark of the Covenant into the fray (1 Sam. 4). This was an entirely superstitious use as they trusted a symbol rather than God. The Ark of the Covenant became the Philistines' idol when they defeated Israel and captured the Ark itself. The Philistines learned that it was worse to deal with Israel's God than just to deal with Israel. Plagues fell upon the people, and in fear they decided to send the Ark back, recognizing God's divine judgment (1 Sam. 6).

A dark period of 20 years with no detailed history followed. Israel seemingly was under Philistine rule, and had no center of worship. Samuel was advancing to manhood and leadership. God's people longed for their lost God and a leader (1 Sam. 7).

Israel Rejected God and Demanded a King

With Israel's continued downfall into evil, the elders came to Samuel and said, "'*Give us a king to judge us.' And Samuel prayed to the Lord. And the Lord said to Samuel, 'Obey the voice of the people in all that they say to you, for they have not rejected you, but they have rejected me from being king over them,'*" (1 Sam. 8:6-7). The new King Saul gained favor for the victories that he won over enemies (1 Sam. 11, 14) but he drew violent criticism for his lack of spiritual leadership for his people under God (1 Sam. 13). Samuel objected to Saul's failures (1 Sam. 15) and declared that a new king would rise up and take Saul's place for Israel. David was anointed by God (1 Sam. 16) and defeated the giant Goliath (1 Sam. 17).

King David Led Israel to God and Unity

Second Samuel is primarily the history of David—a history of his kingship—and gives us a picture of the theocratic monarchy. The people had cried out for a king, and God first gave them Saul after their own hearts. This time, He would give them one after His own heart. David was first anointed king over Judah as a young man (2 Sam. 2). Saul's Northern tribes anointed Saul's son Ish-bosheth their king— dividing Israel. Civil war broke out and David formed alliances from North to South. David's manliness, courage and godliness soon dissolved the Northern opposition, and he became king over the whole, united nation of Israel. King David established a single political and religious headquarters at Jerusalem for both the North and South (2 Sam. 5) and began to establish national worship there with the Ark and Tabernacle (2 Sam. 6).

Philistia still posed military and religious threats to Israel and its new capital. In two major surges King David and his troops crushed the Philistines, and Joshua's incomplete conquest for the Holy Land of Canaan was finally resolved (2 Sam. 5).

David made the city of Jerusalem the religious center of united Israel. With the Ark of the Covenant came pilgrimages, holy day celebrations and memorials of God's faithfulness. These united all of Israel in proper godly worship. David had desires to build the permanent Temple in Jerusalem, but learned from the prophet Nathan that not he, but his offspring, would build the Temple (2 Sam. 7).

The people prospered under their God in this period because they put obedience to God before personal, political, or other interests. This direction was David's priority as his most important speeches encouraged Israel to "put God first." He preached that obedience to God was a prerequisite to a good national life (2 Sam. 23).

David Fell to Idleness, Adultery and Murder

While David's godly heart was right, he was still subject to sin. In a moment of weakness, David went into a downward spiral of sin. He demonstrated idleness, adultery with Bathsheba, cover-up, and murder of her husband Uriah (2 Sam. 11). But as God's king, David had a repentant heart and confessed before his entire nation (2 Sam. 24).

First Chronicles parallels 2 Samuel, but only from the priestly perspective of the royal reign of King David. The Temple priests recorded the genealogies of David and Israel (1 Chron. 1-9), and covered the reign of David from anointing and accession as King (1 Chron. 10-12), bringing back the Ark (1 Chron. 13-17), victories and final conquest over the Philistines (1 Chron. 18-20), preparation for the Temple (1 Chron. 21-27), and his last days (1 Chron. 28-29).

CONSIDER how God picked King David for the people to know God through heart-felt leadership. They knew peace and prosperity through God's provision. They knew sin and punishment by their leader's repentance and God's forgiveness. Consider how you might be called to humbly lead others in a small or mighty way for your Lord God Redeemer!

MAN'S DESTRUCTION AND EXILE

1, 2 KINGS, 2 CHRONICLES

The two books of Kings cover practically all of the period of kingly monarchy over the ancient people of Israel, when the people drifted away from God in political and material desires, and God continually called them back through prophets.

The united kingdom had begun under King David (2 Sam. 5), and continued under King Solomon for 40 years (1 Kings 1-11 and 2 Chron. 1-9). Israel divided under Solomon's successors (1 Kings 12-14) into Israel (North) and Judah (South). Israel fell to Assyria (2 Kings 17) and Judah survived 155 years until falling to Babylonia (2 Kings 25 and 2 Chron. 36). (See Appendix IV, page 255.)

QUESTIONS FOR PERSONAL THOUGHT AND DISCUSSION

1. Read 1 Kings 1:11-14, 28-31—God Used Prophet Nathan to Call and Seat Solomon Next King

a. Whom did Prophet Nathan warn might become king of Israel? (See 1:11-14.) Who had God already anointed as King David's successor? (See 1:13, 28-31.)

b. What was David's advice to Solomon? (See 2:1-4.) God's? (See 6:11-13.) Solomon's prayer? (See 3:9-14.) How did he reign over Israel? (See 11:1-8.)

2. Read 1 Kings 11:9-13, 26-33—God Raised Up Adversaries Against Solomon; Sent a Prophet

a. What was God's reaction to Solomon's sins? (See 11:9-13.) What would happen to Israel and Jerusalem?

b. Who were Jeroboam and Ahijah? (See 11:26-33, 41-43.) Why did God plan to split the kingdom?

c. Read 12:16-24. What command of God did Prophet Shemaiah give to King Rehoboam of Judah?

d. Read 12:25-33. What were some of the sinful acts of King Jeroboam of Israel? (See also 13:33-34.)

e. Read 14:21-24, 29-31. Summarize the reign of King Rehoboam of Judah.

3. Scan 1 Kings 15—Rehoboam Was Followed by Abijam and Asa; Jeroboam by Nadab, Baasha

a. Describe Abijam's reign over Judah. (See 15:3.) Describe Asa's reign over Judah. (See 15:11-14.)

b. Describe Nadab's reign over Israel. (See 15:25-26.) Describe Baasha's reign over Israel. (See 15:33-34.)

4. Read 1 Kings 16:29-34—King Ahab of Israel Brought Israel Into Sin and Decline

a. Describe King Ahab and his reign over Israel. Define Baal worship.

_____

_____

b. Read 18:20-29. Between what "two opinions" did Prophet Elijah confront Israel to choose? How did Baal respond?

_____

c. Read 18:30-40. Describe Elijah's offering and God's response. What impact do you think God's prophet Elijah and the Mt. Carmel miracle had on the people of Israel?

_____

_____

5. Read 2 Chron. 17:1-9, 29:1-11, 34:1-7, 19-21—Jehoshaphat, Hezekiah and Josiah Were Godly

a. Describe King Jehoshaphat's reign over Judah. How did God use him and bless Judah?

_____

_____

b. Describe the reigns of Kings Hezekiah and Josiah over Judah. How did God use them?

_____

6. Read 2 Kings 17:1-8 and 13-18—Israel Captured and Exiled to Assyria in 722 B.C.

a. Why did God's people fail and surrender to their enemies?

b. How did God warn His people of Israel?

c. How would you describe their hearts? (See 17:14-18.)

7. Read 2 Kings 24:1-25:11—Judah Captured and Exiled to Babylon in 597 and 586 B.C.

Why did God's people fail and surrender to these enemies?

8. Read 2 Chron. 36:15-16—God Sent Messengers

a. Who were God's messengers, and what roles did they play?

b. Describe God's compassionate efforts and the response.

Lesson 10 Summary

Man's Destruction and Exile

1, 2 Kings, 2 Chronicles

God Called His Kings and Prophets to Serve Him

The two books of Kings appear in the Hebrew Bible as one book, covering practically all of the period of kingly rule over the ancient people. In Solomon's reign the kingdom reached material magnificence, but began its steep decline into sin. With Solomon's death the united government of the North and South ceased.

First Kings covers a little more than a century and a half, and traces Israel's affluence and influence, through its decline and poverty. Second Kings continues that story covering about three centuries and begins the prophetic period with Elijah (1 Kings 17).

In 2 Chronicles, the view point is of Judah, David's direct heritage, and his "city of God," Jerusalem. Israel is mentioned, but only in relationship to Judah. Kings is simple history, while Chronicles tells the nation's religious life with the temple as the central viewpoint.

CONSIDER how man cannot govern himself with morals and perfect justice—without God. In Israel's government of God, He worked through voices of His prophets with suddenness and clarity. Solomon's government failed because he turned his back on God. And the succession of kings following didn't even approach Solomon's faith.

Consider how God always called His people back. When we listen to Him today, He calls. And when we return to Him He restores us with a transformed life in Christ.

King Solomon Built the Temple at Great Costs

The reign of Solomon was the last of the united kingdom of all Israel. Solomon, a study of contrasts, began his reign with a deep concern for God (1 Kings 3). But he ultimately divided his loyalty between many gods, women and riches (1 Kings 11), and forced labor in the land to meet the building needs (1 Kings 5). He built a great fleet of ships for foreign trade of gold and treasures, and traded with foreign kings to raise money for his projects (1 Kings 9). The nation was ready for rebellion by the time of Solomon's death (1 Kings 12). This began civil opposition between the North (Israel) and the South (Judah).

Kings Rehoboam and Jeroboam Split the Kingdom

Solomon's son Rehoboam became the next autocratic king. The people gathered in discontent and said, *"Thy father made our yoke grievous."* To their complaints he replied, *"whereas my father laid you with a heavy yoke, I will add to your yoke,"* (2 Chron. 10). *"And Judah did what was evil in the sight of the Lord,"* (1 Kings 14). Rehoboam had taken the counsel of wrong advisers (1 Kings 12) and the Northern rebellion was on. *"We have no inheritance in the son of Jesse,"* they said. They appointed Jeroboam king of the North (1 Kings 12) and Judah and Israel became antagonists, even as God's chosen family.

Jeroboam of Israel said to his people that it was too much trouble to go to Jerusalem to worship God, so he encouraged idol worship as an appeal (1 Kings 12). The people had their "religion made easy," became content with their golden calves, and became corrupt.

Neither of these kings trusted in God and both failed equally, eventually leading to the exiles of the divided nation. These books look first at the declining succession of the Northern kings of Israel until their capture and exile to Assyria, and then at the Southern kings of Judah, also declining until their capture and exile to Babylon.

God's Advisers Called His Nation Back to Worship

In appearances and in testimonies of prophets, God governed independently of the kings—as the kings had rejected and forgotten Him. Prophet Ahijah foretold that after Solomon's death the kingdom would be *"rent in twain"*—split apart, and later foretold the death of Jeroboam's son. Shemaiah warned Rehoboam not to fight Jeroboam. A "nameless prophet" prophesied to Jeroboam against the altar. Jehu foretold the fall of Baasha. (See Appendix IV, page 255.)

Elijah, in a dark time of Israel's history, called upon God to speak with fire and rain against the silent Baal gods (1 Kings 18). He proclaimed Him with thunder and rain ending famine. He vindicated Him as the real and only God at Mt. Carmel, and again at Naboth's vinyard. Later, a "son of prophets" rebuked Ahab for allowing Benhadad to escape.

Micaiah, against obstacles, declared the scattering of Israel upon the mountains. Elijah was sent by God to warn His people who their problem and source of trouble were—Ahab and Baal (1 Kings 18). Elijah's successor prophet was Elisha, bringing about a purging of Ahab's house (2 Kings 9).

Kings of Northern Israel Did Evil in God's Eyes

The Kings of Israel to the North were failures in leading God's nation. Israel's history includes the period of civil strife (Jeroboam I - Ahab), of wealth and prosperity (Ahaziah - Jeroboam II) and of rapid decline (Zachariah - Hoshea). Civil Strife resulted from the strained relationship between Israel to the North and Judah to the South. The full-scale civil war was temporarily delayed by the intervention of a prophet (1 Kings 12). But the war soon broke out and the two kingdoms were engaged in war (1 Kings 14). This continued until Syria forced the North and South to ally (1 Kings 22).

A royal marriage between the Northern king's daughter and the Southern king's son sealed that alliance (2 Kings 8), and the civil war ended (1 Kings 22). King Jeroboam I set up worship centers at Dan and Bethel, ensuring loyalty to him as king (1 Kings 12), and permitting worshippers to expand their idols as they chose. He allowed the people to do *"as they saw fit in sin and destruction,"* (1 Kings 13).

Because Israel's kings were no longer anointed by God (1 Kings 15), the throne was typically occupied by murderers protecting their title. Eighteen kings of Israel succeeded Jeroboam I—and none of them followed God. They each *"did what was evil in the sight of the Lord."* Assyria ravished Israel, then conquered Syria, and made Judah a vassal state in the process (2 Chron. 28). Hoshea was put into Assyrian prison (2 Kings 17) and Samaria was put under a three-year siege. The ten tribes of Israel were dispersed to Assyrian captivity and the Northern kingdom of Israel came to an end in 722 B.C. (2 Kings 17).

Kings of Judah Struggled with Baalism

The Kings of Judah following Rehoboam were a succession of 19 kings—but only eight followed God. Judah's history includes civil strife with Rehoboam to Jehoshaphat (2 Chron. 12), Baalism of Jehoram to Queen Athaliah (2 Chron. 18), the *"age of gold"* from Joash to Jotham (2 Kings 11-15), the period of decline from Ahaz to Amon (2 Kings 16-21), reform under Josiah (2 Kings 22), and destruction to the exiles under Jehoahaz to Zedekiah (2 Kings 23-25).

Babylon retaliated and ravaged Jerusalem, tore down the walls, burned the temple, and exiled the remaining Jews to Babylonian captivity (2 Chron. 36). So the remaining Southern kingdom of Judah ended in 586 B.C. *"None remained except the poorest people of the land,"* (2 Kings 24). Zedekiah was appointed by Babylonian King Nebuchadnezzar to rule the poor population remaining in Judah. Zedekiah revolted against the lock hold. God had sent His prophets to speak to deaf ears.

CONSIDER how the Kings and Chronicles focused on building temples and empires, crowning kings and ceremonies, making treaties with foreign nations, commercial development and creative taxation. As the people turned away from God their story is also about wickedness, idol worship, marriage-for-power, murder, and weakness. Consider how we can today look to our Redeemer God as our King even as we live in the world!

RETURN, REBUILD, REFORM AND RESTORE

EZRA, NEHEMIAH, ESTHER AND JOB

After their defeat, God's people from Israel in the North were exiled to Assyria by 722 B.C., and later from Judah territories in the South, to Babylon by 586 B.C. But God would never deny His people full redemption by His covenant promises. In these four books we see God call His people back to Jerusalem—to return, rebuild foundations, reform their ways, and restore relationship with their God.

QUESTIONS FOR PERSONAL THOUGHT AND DISCUSSION

1. Read 2 Chron. 36:17-23 and Ezra 1:1-5— Persian King Cyrus Released the Israelites from Exile

a. Describe in a few words Jerusalem's capture, destruction and exile to Babylon. (See 2 Chron. 36:17-21.)

b. Describe Jeremiah's prophesy of the 70-year exile. (See Jer. 25:8-14.) Describe Cyrus' decree. (See Ezra 1:1-4.)

2. Read Ezra 3:1-11—Offerings and Worship Given

a. Describe the offerings to God in the seventh month, to raise money for re-building. (See 3:6-7.)

b. Describe the Levites' roles and the people's worship. (See 3:8-13.) How many rebuilt the Temple? (See 2:64-70.)

3. Read Ezra 6:13-16—Darius Decreed The Temple Completion; Israel Worshiped with Passover

a. How did God work through the prophets and kings? (See 6:14-15.)

b. How did the offerings and Passover help to return Israel to its covenant with God? (See Ex. 12:24-28.)

c. Read Ezra 7:6-10, 25-28. Why do you think Ezra was picked to come and teach in Israel? Upon whom did Ezra depend? (See 8:21-23.)

4. Read Neh. 1:1-3 and 2:4-8, 17-18—Nehemiah Called by God to Rebuild Jerusalem's Walls

a. Who informed Nehemiah of the demise? Who called him to rebuild the city? (See 2:4-5.)

_____

_____

b. Read 6:15-16. How did the surrounding nations react to the Jerusalem wall?

_____

c. How did Ezra and Nehemiah restore the people's faith? (See 8:1-9.)

_____

5. Read Esther 1:12-19 and 2:1-8, 15-18—Esther Chosen Persian Queen after Vashti is Removed

a. Why was Queen Vashti removed? How and why was Esther, an exiled Jew, selected as the new queen?

_____

_____

b. Why did Esther's cousin Mordecai not bow down to Haman? What was Haman's revenge? (See 3:1-6.)

_____

c. How did Esther save Mordecai and the Jews? (See 7:1-10 and 8:7-8.) What role do you think God had in this rescue?

_____

6. Read Job 1-2:10—Faithful Job Tested by Satan; Lost Property, Children and Health, But Not God

a. Describe Job and his faith. (See 1:1-5.)

_____

_____

b. Read 1:6-12. Why do you think God allowed Satan to test Job? (See also James 1:2-18.)

_____

_____

c. Read 1:20-22 and 2:9-10. How did Job respond to his trials and losses?

_____

_____

7. Read Job 42:1-17—Job Confessed his Faith; Prayed for Doubting Friends; Restored by God

a. How did Job praise God? (See 42:1-6.) How did he help his doubting friends? (See 42:7-9.)

_____

_____

b. How did God restore Job's blessings? Why? (See 42:12-17.)

_____

_____

RETURN, REBUILD, REFORM AND RESTORE

EZRA, NEHEMIAH, ESTHER AND JOB

God Calls His People Back to Himself

After Israel was defeated by Assyria and Babylon to exile, it lost its independence as God's holy nation. By then, under the Persian Empire, God called His people back to Jerusalem—to return to worship, rebuild foundations, reform ways, and restore relationship.

Zerubbabel and Ezra would return the people, rebuild the Temple and restore the laws and statutes. Nehemiah would rebuild the city walls and respect for Jerusalem. Back in Persia, Esther would protect and restore her people under exile. And long before Israel's exile, during Abraham's time, Job never wavered in faith in God during extreme trials—and God restored and rebuilt his broken-but-blessed life.

CONSIDER how God always offers, as He did at the end of the exile, a means of redemption for His people—to return, rebuild foundations, reform ways, and restore relationship in Him. In Ezra we see an opportunity to return to the worship of God, and the will and follow-through to reestablish His statutes. In Nehemiah we see desire to protect God's worship and family—from sinful enemies, from meaningless ritual, and from a weakened people. In Esther we see a quiet, caring and loving God who protects His own, even when they are outside of the protected city walls of Jerusalem. In Job we see a caring and patient God who protects an individual—like you or me—through gain or loss, joy or pain. Job witnessed

his faith to his friends and his God. May we remember
and model in our world these pillars of Gods' story!

These four books conclude the history section of the Old Testament.
Ezra and Nehemiah were a single book in the Hebrew Bible. Esther
lived during the exile during the Persian rule over the Jews, placing the
events near the time of Ezra's return to Jerusalem (Ezra 7). Job, a book
that is also considered poetry, is out of sequence as he lived during the
time of Abraham.

Jews Returned to Rebuild the Temple and City

With an edict issued by Persian King Cyrus, conqueror of Babylon and
King of Persia, Judah was freed and returned to the homeland (Ezra 1).
This first return to Jerusalem from Persian exile allowed thousands of
freed Jews back with their treasures and possessions (Ezra 2, Neh. 7).

Seven months after the first return, led by Zerubbabel, they began to
reconstruct the temple (Ezra 3). A temporary alter to God was built,
workers and materials were solicited, and in the second year the
foundation was laid. The Samaritans, who had occupied Jerusalem
during the exile, were eager to help but the Jews refused.

They retaliated with a plan to slow the building, and construction was
halted (Ezra 4). God persisted through two prophets, Haggai and
Zechariah, who called for quick action. The king overruled and the
work on the temple continued until completion in 515 B.C. (Ezra 6).

Ezra Renewed God's Laws and People's Conduct

The second return was led by Ezra, the priest and scribe (Ezra 7). He
recognized the need for reformed laws (Ezra 7). The temple practices
and sacrifice had become meaningless and routine. Ezra brought law
reform approved by the Persian king as Jerusalem was an autonomous
legal community of the returned exiles (Ezra 7). As Zerubbabel rebuilt
the temple, Ezra restored the spiritual condition of the people. With
God's laws and justice restored, the renewed nation became
independent again as a *"people unto themselves,"* (Neh. 13).

Nehemiah Built City Walls for Safety and Stature

The city of Jerusalem was still without walls which was unsafe and a disgrace to the Jews. Nehemiah, a servant and cupbearer in the Persian king's court, asked to go back to Jerusalem to rebuild the walls (Neh. 2). His request was granted and he returned to Jerusalem to inspect the damaged walls.

Nehemiah led the reconstruction for a renewed Jerusalem (Neh. 3). He faced the same sort of opposition from the Samaritans as Zerubbabel had with the temple, but his people persisted with swords in one hand and brick in the other (Neh. 4). They worked non-stop and in 52 days the wall was rebuilt (Neh. 6).

As Ezekiel had prophesied in a vision, the new Jerusalem and Temple were emerging (Ezek. 40-48). The new Zion as proclaimed by Isaiah was coming (Is. 60-62). The walls of Jerusalem were again strong and complete. Nehemiah concludes the Old Testament history timeline, occurring about 450 years before Jesus' birth.

Esther Used by God to Save the Jews Still in Exile

The book of Esther fits chronologically between the first and second returns to Judah from exile. It provides a picture of the life of Jews who remained in Persia after the first exile. This group of exiled Jews in about 480 B.C. were saved from death by Queen Esther's bravery as God preserved His own people in a foreign land.

Esther, an undisclosed Jewish believer, became the wife of the Persian King Ahasuerus (Esther 2). Haman, the King's Persian commander, plotted to kill all the Jews and targeted the Jew Mordecai, Esther's secret cousin, because he would not bow to Haman, the Persian commander (Esther 3).

Queen Esther confessed to King Ahasuerus her Jewish nationality and pleaded to him to protect the Jews. She revealed Haman's secret plot to murder every Jew (Esther 7). The king had Haman hanged and granted the Jews safe protection in Persia (Esther 8). God's faithfulness, relationship with, and protection of His people—even in their exile—are evident throughout the book, though God's name does not appear.

God Allowed Job to Suffer; Restored Him Two-fold

The book of Job was possibly published about 500 years before Christ, though many scholars date the man back to the times of Genesis and Abraham. He was a prosperous landowner far across the Jordan in Uz.

Job's wealth was from cattle and crops, and he had a large family of ten children. After much success and happiness, Job worried that his children had sinned against God. He was tested by God and Satan, lost his wealth, and became ill (Job 1).

Job's friends said that the illness was due to his own faults—his own sins (Job 3). They expelled him from their town and Job sat alone in misery. Three friends visited him but did not give him much comfort. Job found the way out of his troubles by turning again to God in repentance, hope, and a restored relationship (Job 12).

God challenged Job to trust Him (Job 38), and Job repented fully and prayed for his friends (Job 42). Finally, God replaced two-fold all the wealth Job had at first, and fully restored his relationships—with God and men.

This book is really a story of Job's sufferings and recovery. He was a righteous man and worshipped and obeyed God all his life. He wondered why God allowed him so many sufferings. At last he realized that God was greater and more wonderful than himself, and that God saw well beyond what Job saw, extending mercy and grace.

CONSIDER how God calls us back to Himself even when we leave to exiled lives of bondage and pain. Consider how He helps us rebuild and restore our life with Him, and in concert with others. Think about how in Jesus Christ we are redeemed like Job, honored like Queen Esther, empowered like Ezra and sustained like Nehemiah. Consider asking your Creator today how He might restore you in His Light and blessings!

WORSHIP, WISDOM, PREACHING AND SONG

PSALMS, PROVERBS, ECCLESIASTES, AND SONG OF SOLOMON

These books help us worship our God and Lord, as they helped Kings David, Solomon and many others throughout the ages. They can inspire us with meaningful illustrations, petitions, litanies and praises as God has heard these prayers from the mighty and meek alike. Within them we find wisdom, nurture, comfort and joy in our Creator and Redeemer.

QUESTIONS FOR PERSONAL THOUGHT AND DISCUSSION

1. Read Psalms 23, 139, 32 and 51—Personal and Penitent Psalms

a. What do you find most personal in Psalms 23 and 139? What connects most to your own life?

b. How might the "penitent" psalms help a person be rid of sin and guilt? How did David recommend repentance? (See 51:13-14.) How could these verses help you in understanding and receiving God's forgiveness?

2. Read Psalms 55 and 92— Psalms of Praise and Thanksgiving

What ways could you find in these two Psalms for you to be more thankful? When in 92:1-4 is the Psalmist thankful?

3. Scan Psalm 22 and Read 110—Psalms of Messianic Prophesy

a. What prophesies of the Messiah can you find in Psalm 22? (See also Matt. 27:31, 35, 41, 43, and 46.)

b. What prophesies of Christ can you find in David's Psalm 110? (See also Matt. 22:44, Heb. 7:14-17.)

c. How do you think these prophecies helped Israel's relationship with God? In what ways might they help you in your relationship with God?

4. Read Prov. 1:1-19—The Purposes of Proverbs

a. What are a few ways we might benefit from the Proverbs in 1:1-7?

_____

_____

b. What are some warnings we find in 1:8-19?

_____

_____

5. Scan Prov. 22—Proverbs of Wisdom

a. How might God give wisdom, knowledge, and even our words? When might He grant wisdom? (See 22:17-19.)

_____

_____

b. Write in your own words the wisdom you find in Prov. 22:6, 17-19.

_____

_____

c. Read Prov. 31:10-31. Think of a God-fearing woman you admire and note some of her godly traits from these verses.

_____

_____

6. Read Eccles. 1:12-18—Preaching in Ecclesiastes

a. Who is the preacher and what is his experience in seeking wisdom? (See also Eccles. 1:1.)

b. Compare Eccles. 1:13-18 with Gen. 3:22-24. How do God and Solomon each describe the difficulty of knowledge? How can Christ resolve this difficulty?

7. Read Song of Sol. 7:10-13 and 1 Cor. 11:1-3— The Parallel Love Story of Christ and His Church

a. If Paul is describing Solomon's "Song," who are the key characters in the parallel stories? (See also Rev. 19:7-10.)

b. Read Song of Sol. 8:5-6 and 2 Tim. 2:19. Compare the "awakening" and seal in each.

WORSHIP, WISDOM, PREACHING AND SONG

PSALMS, PROVERBS, ECCLESIASTES, AND SONG OF SOLOMON

The Psalms Guide Us in Worship and Praise

The book of Psalms alone can be described as a book of worship, including wisdom, preaching and song. It is so diverse and long that it is covered, used and described in many other ways as well. We point to these four descriptions in the Psalms first, and then look separately to Proverbs as the "wisdom" book, Ecclesiastes as "preaching," and at the "Song" of Solomon. Job, from our last lesson, is often grouped stylistically with these books together as the Bible's books of literature, but also fits into the history of early Genesis.

CONSIDER David's Psalm 19. Verses 1 and 14 read, *"The heavens declare the glory of God, and the sky above proclaims his handiwork,"* and *"Let the words of my mouth and the meditation of my heart be acceptable in your sight, O Lord, my rock and my redeemer."* Consider how David humbly praises his Creator in many beautiful, personal and diverse ways before asking for God's provision of wisdom, words, and heart-felt meditation. Consider giving praises to your Creator before you

make heart-felt petitions, and, like David, consider standing before your Rock and Redeemer Jesus Christ.

The Psalms together are a book of worship. "Psalm" is the Greek word for "poem set to music." The Hebrew word was simply "praises" or book of praises. It was the worship book, or "hymnal" of the Hebrew people. We have no proof who the editor was, but many psalms are "of David," and were assembled during, near, or soon after his time. This was a period of extensive publishing during the reign of Solomon (along with the next three books that are in this lesson).

Other psalms were authored by Solomon, Asaph, and Moses. The final editing probably took place during the time of Ezra, thus the dates range through many centuries. The authors and editor were very familiar with the Pentateuch. They were used frequently at festivals and special occasions such as the Feast of Booths. They were liturgical for ancient times, just as they are today in the life of the church. They cover a range of human emotions before God, like cries of anguish to heavenly praises worshiping God. They fall into three broad groups: personal and penitent; praise, liturgy and thanksgiving; and prophesy of the Messiah. Personal Psalms include 23, 27, 34, 37, 55 and 139. Penitent Psalms include 32, 51, and 130. Praise Psalms include: liturgical, 120 and 135; praise, 18, 100, and 103; and thanksgiving, 66 and 92. Prophetic and Messianic Psalms include 2, 22, 45 and 110.

The Proverbs Give Us Practical Wisdom

Proverbs is the book of practical wisdom. As it is one of the "wisdom" books of the Hebrew people, the word wisdom occurs frequently and is synonymous with knowledge, understanding, and discretion. The book always takes for granted the wisdom of God, and seeks to instruct man on what godly wisdom really is.

A proverb is a short, pithy saying, or "soundbite," focusing on a comparison or antithesis. These proverbs are aimed at giving an outline of ethical regulations for everyday life, much as a preacher might aid his congregation with practical sermons for godly living.

Two examples are from Proverbs 14:1-2, which read, *"The wisest of women builds her house, but folly with her own hands tears it down. Whoever walks in uprightness fears the Lord, but he who is devious in his ways despises him."* The underlying reference is that of God Himself, the all-wise giver of wisdom. Man is only wise as he recognizes, receives and follows the wisdom of God. The word proverb translates closely to "likeness," like a parable. It is to be in the likeness of God's wisdom.

Proverbs include those for children (Prov. 1), for seeking wisdom (Prov. 1-3), for parents (Prov. 4-9), for living godly lives (Prov. 10-24), for relationships (Prov. 25-30), and for leaders and women (Prov. 31).

Solomon authored much of the book, but its origins spanned more time than his life. Some portions were compiled by Hezekiah's scribes, while the last two chapters were written by Agur and Lemuel. The book was completed and published around 700 B.C.

Ecclesiastes Preaches Against Vanity and For Godly Wisdom

Ecclesiastes means "preacher," "teacher," or "assembly," and is the book of preaching against materialism and folly. The book is written in a direct, matter-of-fact way, from both the preacher's personal experiences and the observations of others. He shows that life's wholeness can only be found in the spiritual, not merely in the material. The book preaches on experiencing vanity (Eccles. 1-2), observing vanity (Eccles. 3-6), living with vanity (Eccles. 7-9), and finding wisdom (Eccles. 10-12).

Traditionally ascribed to Solomon, Ecclesiastes may have reflected the thinking of his later years, and only the first section has evidence of Solomon's authorship. Ecclesiastes 1:1-5 reads, *"The words of the Preacher, the son of David, king in Jerusalem. Vanity of vanities, says the Preacher, vanity of vanities! All is vanity. What does man gain by all the toil at which he toils under the sun? A generation goes, and a generation comes, but the earth remains forever. The sun rises, and the sun goes down, and hastens to the place where it rises."*

Song of Solomon is the Love Song of the Bible

There are commonly two very diverse interpretations of this song. One is of an "emotional man-to-woman" Eastern love song. The second is of a portrayal of Christ's love to His church. It is clear that, no matter if one or both are true, Solomon did not see the prophecy of the church, even if he spoke the words in the hidden song. Alongside these two stories is the relationship that exists between Jehovah and Israel. It is possible that Solomon had this intention in mind. The Jewish prophets could present to him this story while hiding the coming prophesy of Christ and His church. These scenes of the love song include wooing, winning, and the relationship of the bride and groom.

In viewing the relationship between Jehovah and Israel, and thinking about the coming relationship between Christ and His church, we see that the love stories pictured are an idyllic vision. That perfection can really only be experienced with God, and between Christ and His church. The writer symbolizes the love of Jehovah and Israel, and that of a man and a woman. Since marriage is ordained by God for man and woman, it is as Israel, the woman figure, seeks her Groom. Jehovah. Song 3:1-3 reads, *"On my bed by night I sought him whom my soul loves; I sought him, but found him not. I will rise now and go about the city, in the streets and in the squares; I will seek him whom my soul loves. I sought him, but found him not. The watchmen found me as they went about in the city. 'Have you seen him whom my soul loves?'"*

CONSIDER how God provides the means to worship, praise, teach, and learn His wisdom—all for our relationship in Him. Consider how these worship books are timeless sources of praise and wisdom for mankind, and lead us to Jesus Christ. Consider a time when you might read through these books, journaling your personal growth in godly wisdom and understanding.

POINTING AHEAD TO CHRIST, JUDGMENT AND PEACE

ISAIAH

Isaiah gave the people of Judah warnings (Isaiah 1-39) and of hope (40-66). He pronounced God's judgment on the nation, and then expanded the message to the judgment of other sinful nations. The best news of the prophets comes when Isaiah consoled the people with God's promises of the Messiah Savior. Yahweh God, he said, is the all-powerful Savior who will come to rescue His people.

QUESTIONS FOR PERSONAL THOUGHT AND DISCUSSION

1. Scan Isaiah 1—Isaiah Warned of Wickedness

a. Who was Isaiah? (See also 2 Pet. 1:20-21.) Where was he located and who were the kings? (See verse 1.)

b. In a few words, what was the state of Judah? (See 1:2-31.)

2. Read Isaiah 6:8-13—God Commissioned Isaiah

a. Describe the conversation between God and Isaiah. (See 6:8-10.) Why would the peoples' hearts be dulled?

b. Read 6:11-13, 8:1-10, and 10:20-23. Describe the vision of the exiled Jerusalem, conquering by Assyria, and return.

3. Read Isaiah 9:1-7 and 11:1-5, 10—For Unto Us a Child is Born

a. How explicit was Isaiah's prophesy? Give examples. (See 9:1-7 and Luke 2:11.)

b. Who was Jesse? Why was this important to the story of Christ? (See 11:1-5, 10 and Acts 13:22-23.)

4. Read Isaiah 25:7-9 and Rev. 21:1-4—Mt. Zion and the New Jerusalem

Compare Isaiah's Mt. Zion and Jerusalem prophesy to John's New Jerusalem vision.

_____

_____

5. Read Isaiah 30:18:22—The Lord Is Gracious

Describe God and Christ in Isaiah's terms. What will the redeemed say after they reject their idols?

_____

6. Read Isaiah 32:1-8 and 9:7—God Will Send a Righteous King

Compare King Jesus' righteousness to that of David's throne.

_____

_____

7. Read Isaiah 44:1-8—Israel was Chosen for a King, a Rock, a Redeemer

a. Describe how Israel was chosen for God the Redeemer King.

_____

_____

b. Describe Jesus' uniqueness and future reign as King of Israel. (See also John 17:1-4.)

8. Read Isaiah 51:3, 15-16—Zion Restored to Eden

How will the new Zion compare to the Eden garden? (See 51:3, Gen. 2:8-9 and Rev. 22:1-4.)

9. Read Isaiah 52:13-53:12—He Was Despised, Rejected and Pierced for Our Transgressions

a. Find several descriptions of Christ at His crucifixion, and reasons Isaiah gives for His death.

b. Review 53:10-12. Using Isaiah's vision, describe God's gift of sacrificing Christ, the reasons and purposes.

LESSON 13 SUMMARY

POINTING AHEAD TO CHRIST, JUDGMENT AND PEACE

ISAIAH

God Used Prophets to Give Warnings and Hope

The Bible's prophets actually cover most of the Old Testament—from Abraham, Moses, Samuel, Nathan, Elijah and Elisha—to Haggai, Zechariah and Malachi after the exiles. Isaiah is perhaps the most noted prophet as his writings carry both his name (termed a literary prophet) and the most revealed promises of Christ the Messiah.

Isaiah is also referred to as a "major" prophet, along with Jeremiah, Ezekiel and Daniel—because of the length and number of prophesies recorded. Isaiah prophesied to Southern Judah along with Jeremiah, Joel, Micah, Habakkuk, and Zephaniah. Obadiah prophesied to Edom, Hosea and Amos to Northern Israel, and Jonah and Nahum to Assyria.

During the exile (605-535 B.C.), Ezekiel and Daniel prophesied to the people of Israel in Babylon. After the exile, Haggai, Zechariah and Malachi prophesied to Jerusalem and broader Judah.

CONSIDER how God always calls His people back with messages of hope and promise, even in the midst of popular sin and unholy secular governments. Consider how Isaiah points to both failures and hope, as a loving parent would point a child to the likelihood and dangers of personal failures, as well as hope in the life ahead. Consider how your God delivered your Christ Redeemer as promised by the prophet Isaiah, and blessed you to be a blessing for the world just as He promised to Abraham centuries ago. May you be the blessing today that He has blessed you to be in Jesus Christ!

False prophets also existed (see Jer. 14:13-16; 2 Pet. 2:1-3), and tried to be popular with the kings by telling them and the people what they wanted to hear. False prophets wanted God to fulfill their "prophetic" ideas spoken. In every generation there are false and true prophetic voices—who speak God's truth or man's lies and distortions.

True prophets were chosen, anointed, appointed and empowered by God (see also 2 Pet. 1:20-21). Generally, they were common workers or "lay-persons"—called out by God to speak His truth against sin.

Isaiah Was Called by God to Promise the Messiah

Isaiah, the first book of the literary prophets, was commissioned by God to "see" for the kings of Judah, and all people who will read these prophesies. Isaiah 6:8 reads, *"And I heard the voice of the Lord saying, 'Whom shall I send, and who will go for us?' Then I said, 'Here I am! Send me.' And he said, 'Go, and say to this people: 'Keep on hearing, but do not understand; keep on seeing, but do not perceive.'"*

In the study of Kings we saw "oral" prophets who spoke to the historical moments in which they lived—such as Elijah and Elisha. They warned against the Baalism of Ahab's era. Isaiah and Jeremiah also spoke to current events in Judah and all of Israel. They spoke their God-sent messages to the past, current and future. When the nation was morally broken, they urged the king and people the dangers of sin. Isaiah told the people of Judah the impending truth about its future.

Isaiah 1:5-6 reads, *"Why will you still be struck down? Why will you continue to rebel? The whole head is sick, and the whole heart faint. From the sole of the foot even to the head, there is no soundness in it, but bruises and sores and raw wounds; they are not pressed out or bound up or softened with oil."*

Isaiah described a bleak future for those who held their confidence in sinful things. Isaiah 1:28 reads, *"But rebels and sinners shall be broken together, and those who forsake the Lord shall be consumed."* He offered difficult words for those who wouldn't turn from sin, but he also gave hope to those who would listen and honor their God.

Isaiah 6:13 reads, *"And though a tenth remain in it, it will be burned again, like a terebinth or an oak, whose stump remains when it is felled. The holy seed is its stump."* Isaiah 11:1-2 picks up with this prophesy of King David's father in Christ's lineage, *"There shall come forth a shoot from the stump of Jesse, and a branch from his roots shall bear fruit. And the Spirit of the Lord shall rest upon him, the Spirit of wisdom and understanding, the Spirit of counsel and might, the Spirit of knowledge and the fear of the Lord."*

Isaiah Promised the Birth of the Christian Era

The Davidic Kingdom, Isaiah said, would never end. As he encouraged them, Israel gladly looked for the birth of a new era under a new King. Isaiah 32:1 reads, *"Behold, a king will reign in righteousness, and princes will rule in justice."*

The people dreamed of a renovation of the holy city Jerusalem that King David set up as the center of God's worship (2 Sam. 6). Isaiah called this the "exaltation of Mt. Zion." Isaiah 2:1-3 reads, *"The word that Isaiah the son of Amoz saw concerning Judah and Jerusalem. It shall come to pass in the latter days that the mountain of the house of the Lord shall be established as the highest of the mountains, and shall be lifted up above the hills; and all the nations shall flow to it, and many peoples shall come, and say: 'Come, let us go up to the mountain of the Lord, to the house of the God of Jacob, that he may teach us his ways and that we may walk in his paths.' For out of Zion shall go forth the law, and the word of the Lord from Jerusalem."*

The exalted Jerusalem was to be all-inclusive. David's rule had been limited to the chosen family of Abraham, but the new kingdom would embrace all the nations of the earth. Isaiah 49:6 says, *"It is too light a thing that you should be my servant to raise up the tribes of Jacob and to bring back the preserved of Israel; I will make you as a light for the nations, that my salvation may reach to the end of the earth."*

Isaiah Prophesied the New Zion and Redeemer

Isaiah spoke to the covenant of Abraham, promising that their Eden paradise would be restored with the peoples' repentance and righteousness (Isaiah 51:3). These covenant promises for Israel were conditional, as God promised redemption for the righteous followers. Only a sanctified and redeemed remnant of Israel would receive the Redeemer and Savior (Isaiah 52:8-10).

The offer of hope would be completed by a new King who would suffer as a servant leader. Isaiah 52:12-13 reads, *"For you shall not go out in haste, and you shall not go in flight, for the Lord will go before you, and the God of Israel will be your rear guard. Behold, my servant shall act wisely; he shall be high and lifted up, and shall be exalted."*

Isaiah continued the crucifixion prophesy with 53:3-6, *"He was despised and rejected by men, a man of sorrows and acquainted with grief; and as one from whom men hide their faces he was despised, and we esteemed him not. Surely he has borne our griefs and carried our sorrows; yet we esteemed him stricken, smitten by God, and afflicted. But he was pierced for our transgressions; he was crushed for our iniquities; upon him was the chastisement that brought us peace, and with his wounds we are healed. All we like sheep have gone astray; we have turned—every one—to his own way; and the Lord has laid on him the iniquity of us all."*

CONSIDER how God called Isaiah to warn His people of wickedness—and give them hope for the completed covenant they had dreamed of since Abraham. For the people to receive this new covenant, they would have to believe the prophet and their God. Consider how the revealed and completed prophesies confirm God's promises and give us the assurance of our Christ Redeemer. Praise Him for His deliverance for His people!

POINTING AHEAD TO FAILURE AND FUTURE

JEREMIAH, LAMENTATIONS, EZEKIEL AND DANIEL

The books of prophets Jeremiah, Ezekiel and Daniel show us three men of God whom He called, appointed and commissioned to communicate His messages with the kings and people of Israel. They show us a just God who has delayed His judgment over a sinful and rebellious people. Jeremiah preached during Jerusalem darkest days, and wrote Lamentations for the fallen Jerusalem. Ezekiel and Daniel were deported to Babylon in exile and became God's mouthpieces to the Kings of Babylon and God's people.

QUESTIONS FOR PERSONAL THOUGHT AND DISCUSSION

1. Read Jer. 1:1-10 and 2:1-9—God Called Jeremiah Before Birth

a. How and when do you think God planned Jeremiah's role as a prophet to Judah? (See 1:4-9.) What roles did Jeremiah play? (See 1:10.)

b. How did God put the words into Jeremiah's mouth, and what was the message to Jerusalem? (See 2:1-9 and 2 Pet. 1:21.)

2. Read Jer. 31:31-34, 32:36-41 and Heb. 8:1-13— Jeremiah Prophesied the New Covenant

a. Describe the new covenant. (See 31:33-34 and 32:36-41.)

_____

_____

b. Describe the new covenant in Hebrews. (See Heb. 8:6-7.) Why and how is it better?

_____

_____

3. Read Lam. 1:1-8 and 3:22-27—Jeremiah Lamented Suffering and Praised His Lord

a. What was Jerusalem's downfall? (See 1:7-8.)

_____

_____

b. Compare the "lamentations" in 3:1-20 with the "praises" in 3:21-27.

_____

_____

c. Read Lam. 3:58-66. Describe Jeremiah's hope and faith in his Lord.

_____

4. Read Ezek. 36:1-27 and Rom 3:19-26—Ezekiel Prophesied a New Heart and a New Spirit

a. For what did God seek vindication? What did God offer that would lead His people to follow His statutes and rules?

b. What comes through the law? (See Rom. 3:19-20.)

c. In Christ, how are we justified? (See Rom. 3:21-26.)

5. Read Ezek. 37:1-14—Ezekiel and the Dry Bones

a. Compare Ezek. 37:5-6 with Gen 2:7 and note similarities.

b. Read Ezek. 37:12-14 and 1 Thess. 4:13-18. Note similarities.

5. Read Dan. 1:1-21—Daniel Deported from Judah

a. Describe, from Daniel's account, the final exile. (See 1:1-7.)

b. Describe Daniel's faithfulness to his God, and how he accomplished permission to honor his beliefs. (See 1:8-16.)

c. How did God use Daniel in Israel's exile? (See 1:17-21.)

6. Read Dan. 2:1-45—Daniel Interpreted Dreams

a. What did Daniel do before his appointment with the king? (See 2:16-18.)

b. What was God's response to Daniel, and Daniel's response to God? (See 2:19-23.)

c. Read verse 44. Whose is the Kingdom that shall never be destroyed? What kingdoms were destroyed after this king?

POINTING AHEAD TO FAILURE AND FUTURE

JEREMIAH, LAMENTATIONS, EZEKIEL AND DANIEL

God Called His People Back Through Prophets

The books of prophets Jeremiah, Ezekiel and Daniel reveal a patient and holy God who has delayed judgment over a sinful and rebellious people. Jeremiah faithfully ministered in spite of persecution, and when Judah's downfall finally came he wrote his Lamentations as a funeral message for fallen Jerusalem.

Jeremiah's contemporary Ezekiel prepared the exiled people for religious reconstruction in Babylon. Daniel was deported to Babylon as well, and became God's servant-prophet to the kings of Babylon, protecting God's people in exile and serving as His mouthpiece.

CONSIDER how God commissioned ordinary people as His prophets for Israel and Judah—before, after and during the exiles to Assyria and Babylon. Consider how in our most difficult times—personally, as families and nationally—God continually calls and commissions leaders to bring us His wisdom and hope amid our difficulties. Think of times when you needed God most, and He sent you wisdom and hope of what your Redeemer and Savior will do in your life. Consider how He blesses you to be a blessing to others as part of the covenant with Abraham and New Covenant of Jesus Christ. Listen for His words for when He may be blessing you to be a blessing to others in His great Name.

Jeremiah Gave His Prophesies and Lamentations

Jeremiah was consecrated before he was born, and as a youth appointed a prophet to the nations. He said in Jer. 1:4, *"Now the word of the LORD came to me, saying, 'Before I formed you in the womb I knew you, and before you were born I consecrated you; I appointed you a prophet to the nations.'"*

The exile to Babylon, and subsequent freedom by the Persian King Cyrus, was a direct fulfillment, or "sign," for the people to witness God's truth through the prophets, and also God's judgments through His actions. With the institutions of their religious faith swept away, the Holy Land devastated, and Jerusalem and the temple in ruins, the people of Judah found themselves crying in despair.

Jeremiah wrote in his Lamentations (Lam. 2:11): *"My eyes are spent with weeping; my stomach churns; my bile is poured out to the ground because of the destruction of the daughter of my people, because infants and babies faint in the streets of the city."* And 3:17-18, *"My soul is bereft of peace; I have forgotten what happiness is; so I say, "My endurance has perished; so has my hope from the Lord."*

Jeremiah recorded his prophesies to Judah in the form of sermons. He preached on the condemnation of Judah (Jer. 2-25), his own conflicts (Jer. 26-29), future restoration of Jerusalem (Jer. 30-33), the fall and condition of Jerusalem (Jer. 34-45), prophesies to Gentile nations (Jer. 46-51), and the record of Jerusalem's fall and exile (Jer. 52).

The judgment God laid upon Judah in exile was a sign for all to see, and a warning for judgment of all the world and all its peoples. Feeling abandoned, Jeremiah and all Israel remembered their past strength in the promise of hope. God had not abandoned His people. Jeremiah gave hope as he spoke of the new era that Israel's remnant would discover (Jer. 31) and prophesied the coming Shepherd and Righteous Branch to be called *"the Lord our Righteousness"* (Jer. 23:1-8).

Ezekiel Deported to Babylon in Second Exile

Ezekiel was younger than Jeremiah and Daniel, but was their contemporary. After having known Jeremiah in Jerusalem, he was carried to Babylon in captivity in a later exile after that of Daniel. Ezekiel was from a family of priests. He had a wife and home, and served and preached in ministry for 20 years. His name means *"God strengthens"* as he illustrated that his strength came from God.

King Nebuchadnezzar destroyed Jerusalem in three attacks, in 605, 597 and 586 B.C. Daniel was among the first group exiled in 605, and Ezekiel was in the second group in 597 B.C. Jeremiah went to Egypt.

Ezekiel's main burden was God's wrath and judgment against sin. He focused on Judah's sin-led doom (Ezek. 1-25), and that of the neighboring sinful nations (Ezek. 26-32). He foretold the restoration of Israel and its blessings to come (Ezek. 33-48).

He prophesied with parables, logic and symbolism. An example is "birth" in Ezek. 16:4, *"And as for your birth, on the day you were born your cord was not cut, nor were you washed with water to cleanse you, nor rubbed with salt, nor wrapped in swaddling cloths."*

Ezekiel prophesied the fall of Jerusalem (Ezek. 7). After it fell the people flocked to hear him as he spoke with the authority and knowledge of God. With their trust and attention he later assured the people of God's restoration and hope for the future (Ezek. 40-48).

Ezekiel prophesied the coming of the True Shepherd (Ezek. 31:11-16). He spoke for God saying, *"I myself will be the shepherd of my sheep, and I myself will make them lie down, declares the Lord God. I will seek the lost, and I will bring back the strayed, and I will bind up the injured, and I will strengthen the weak, and the fat and the strong I will destroy. I will feed them in justice."*

He prophesied a covenant of peace and blessings, saying, *"I will make with them a covenant of peace and banish wild beasts from the land, so that they may dwell securely in the wilderness and sleep in the woods. And I will make them and the places all around my hill a blessing, and I will send down the showers in their season; they shall be showers of blessing,"* (Ezek. 31:25-26).

Daniel Taken to Babylon in First Exile

Daniel prophesied future events such as a period of Gentile ascendancy in the church age. The book is written in Aramaic and Hebrew—the Aramaic portion for the Gentile nations even before Christ proclaimed the gospel was for them—and the Hebrew was written for the Jews. God's intervention is shown in the well-known stories of the fiery furnace (Dan. 3), in the fall, and repentance, of Nebuchadnezzar (Dan. 4), and in the lions' den (Dan. 6).

After his rescue by God from the lions, he wrote, *"Then King Darius wrote to all the peoples, nations, and languages that dwell in all the earth: 'Peace be multiplied to you. I make a decree, that in all my royal dominion people are to tremble and fear before the God of Daniel, for he is the living God, enduring forever; his kingdom shall never be destroyed, and his dominion shall be to the end. He delivers and rescues; he works signs and wonders in heaven and on earth, he who has saved Daniel from the power of the lions.' So this Daniel prospered during the reign of Darius and the reign of Cyrus the Persian."*

In these revelations of God's promises, Daniel gave a great sign through King Cyrus in 538 B.C., as prophesied by Jeremiah (Jer. 25 and Ezra 1). The even greater sign of Christ's birth would come 538 years later with the Messiah King and Savior!

CONSIDER how in the exile times, God's justice required judgment—just as actions today have consequences. As we saw with the Judges, God's justice focused on judgment and redemption according to His laws. Consider how a world without God's laws, systems of justice, mercy and forgiveness—is a world of chaos filling the moral void, lacking relationship with God and others. Praises that just as God created your world today, you and your contemporaries are subject to His truth and justice, and are offered His mercy and grace of Christ the Redeemer!

POINTING AHEAD TO HOPE AND FUTURE

MINOR PROPHETS HOSEA - MALACHI

The 12 minor prophets, now a group of shorter books bearing their names, were once in a single scroll. They include nine who prophesied during the declines: Hosea and Amos to Israel in the North (2 Kings 14); Obadiah to Edom (2 Kings 8); Joel, Micah, Habakkuk and Zephaniah to Judah in the South (2 Kings 12-23); and Jonah and Nahum to Assyria (2 Kings 13, 21). Three prophesied in Jerusalem and broader Judah after the exile: Haggai, Zechariah and Malachi (Ezra 5, 13). Other prophets include "oral" prophets and "major" prophets (see pages 113-114 and Appendix IV, page 255.)

QUESTIONS FOR PERSONAL THOUGHT AND DISCUSSION

1. Read Hos. 1:1-11—Hosea's Family Was a Vision

Compare his family in 1:2-8 with Israel in 1:10-11.

2. Read Joel 2:26-29, 31-32—Joel Foretold Holy Spirit at Pentecost, Christ's Second Coming

a. Compare 2:28-29 with Acts 2:1-4. Note similarities.

b. Compare 2:30-32 with Rev. 6:12-16 and Matt. 24:29-31.

3. Read Amos 2:4-16—Amos Told of Judgments

a. What were Judah's transgressions? (See 2:4-5.)

b. What were Israel's transgressions? (See 2:6-16.)

4. Read Obadiah :10-12, :18—Judgment of Edom

Why did God use His wrath against Edom?

5. Read Jonah 1:1-3, 12-17—A Mission to Nineveh

a. Why do you think Jonah avoided God's call to Nineveh?

b. Read Jonah 3. What resulted when he followed God?

6. Read Micah 5:1-4—Christ's Birth in Bethlehem

Compare 5:1-4 with Matt. 2:1-6, detailing his prophesy.

7. Read Nahum 2:2, 8-13—Nineveh Will Perish

What were God's reasons for destroying Nineveh?

8. Read Hab. 1:1-17—God Will Bring Salvation

a. List questions Habakkuk asks God. (See 1:1-4, 12-17.)

b. Summarize God's answers. (See 1:5-11 and 2:2-6.)

9. Read Zeph. 1:1-3, 14—The Great Day of the Lord

a. Compare Zeph. 1:1-3 with Matt.13:41-43.

b. Compare Zeph. 1:14-15 with Matt 24:29-31.

10. Read Haggai 2:1-9—Prophesies for All Nations

a. Compare 2:6-7 to Luke 24:44-47. What do you think *"all nations, beginning from Jerusalem"* refers to?

b. How do you think the Great Commission might fulfill the covenant with Abraham in Gen. 12-1-3?

11. Read Zech. 1:1-6, 8:20-23—Restoring Worship

a. When did God call Zechariah? Describe his vision for worship in Jerusalem.

b. Compare Zech. 4:1-6 with Rev. 1:10-20. How does Zechariah's vision compare to John's vision?

12. Read Mal. 3:1-2—God Previews Christ's Arrival

Compare Mal. 3:1-2 with Luke 7:24-27. In Jesus' words, what did Malachi mean in his prophesy?

LESSON 15 SUMMARY

POINTING AHEAD TO HOPE AND FUTURE

MINOR PROPHETS HOSEA - MALACHI

God Sent Messages through His Prophets

All of the 16 literary prophets—of major (4 longer) and minor (12 shorter) designation—carried the same, basic four messages: 1. God calls out the sinful practices of His people, and exposes other nations; 2. God calls His people back to His justice, truth, worship, repentance, obedience, mercy and grace; 3. God is sovereign and just, and will bring justice and consequences in His timing; and 4. God's purposes will be fulfilled in a Messianic age of salvation, worship and peace.

Hosea Used His Family's Sin as Israel's Warning

Hosea's name means "salvation." Instead of trusting God, Israel had tried to buy the favor of Assyria and Egypt. They kept the name of God, but used the rituals of Baal worship. Hosea symbolically prophesied to Israel's harlotry against God through his marriage to Gomer, whom he portrayed as a faithless harlot in a land that *"commits great whoredom by forsaking the Lord,"* (Hos.1:2). He forgave Gomer and paid her prostitution debts (Hos. 3), illustrating God's forgiveness and His redemption of Israel (Hos. 11-14).

CONSIDER how God constantly sends His people into the world armed with His truth, laws and covenant blessings. But, as with Adam and Eve, they fall to the world's lies, sins and apostasy. But also consider how God constantly calls His people back. He reminds them of His promises of old, and how His Messiah Savior will return them to His image that they were designed to bear. Praises that our Redeemer has already shed His blood in our stead!

Joel Prophesied the Coming of the Holy Spirit

Joel's name means "Yahweh is God" and he was very acquainted with Judah and Jerusalem. His prophesies focused on God's judgment of Judah and warning signs of future disaster with the illustration of a locust invasion (Joel 1). Most remarkably, he prophesied the outpouring of the Holy Spirit at Pentecost (Joel 2, Acts 2).

Amos Foretold the Judgment, Restoration of Israel

Amos means "burden-bearer." A herdsman and wood-cutter, he lived in Judah and prophesied the judgments on the divided Israel and Judah (Amos 2). He continued to speak for God to Israel through their worship center in Bethel and in a proclamation of hope in God he foretold its restoration from ruin (Amos 9:11-15).

Obadiah Prophesied God's Judgment on Edom

Obadiah means "servant of Yahweh" and his focus was the evil, destruction and extinction of Edom, the descendants of Esau. Obadiah's prophesies judged Edom for its cruel conduct toward God's people (Obad. :1-9). In the day of Zion, Obadiah said, Israel would conquer its conquerors and expand itself to be the Lord's kingdom (Obad. :21).

Jonah Was an Unwilling Missionary to Nineveh

Jonah means "dove," as one who would bring the good news home reflecting Noah and Christ (Matt. 12, Luke 11). Nineveh, the capital of the empire Assyria, represented defiance against God. The book is Jonah's biography illustrating God's concern for saving all nations. Jonah was unwilling to go to Nineveh as God called him (Jonah 1), representing a disobedient nation. When faced with judgment in the fish, he prayed (Jonah 2), and was released in Nineveh (Jonah 3), where he preached repentance, judgment and mercy (Jonah 3-4).

Micah Prophesied the Birthplace of Christ

Micah means "who is like Yahweh?" He lived outside Jerusalem where traders passed in route to Egypt, and witnessed the corruptive influence of foreign nations. He pleaded with God's people for morality, with little regard for politics (Micah 1-3). He prophesied the birth of Christ in Bethlehem (Micah 5) and asked the people, *"what does the Lord require of you?"* (Micah 6).

Nahum Prophesied Nineveh's Fall to Babylon

Nahum means "comfort." Many years after Jonah ministered to Nineveh, Nahum again preached against its ruthless military power and dishonest commerce (Nah. 3). He promoted God's power, comfort and refuge. Nahum prophesied the downfall of Nineveh, though it was a seemingly invincible fortress city. This came true when the Tigris River overflowed the walls allowing a complete Babylonian invasion.

Habakkuk Questioned God, Heard His Answers

Habakkuk's ministry, before Judah's invasion by the Chaldeans, gives a dialogue with God on why oppression and wickedness are unpunished. In this Q-and-A format, God answered that He used the Chaldeans to punish the Jewish oppressors (Hab. 1). He prophesied that the people of God will possess the earth, the righteous shall live by faith (Hab. 2), and God brings joy in salvation (Hab. 3).

Zephaniah Prophesied the Day of the Lord

Zephaniah means "he whom Yahweh protected." He announced Judah's approaching judgment by the Chaldeans (Zeph. 1), and gave hope as he foretold God's deliverance and restoration of all Israel (Zeph. 3). He prophesied the Day of the Lord—Christ's second coming—quoted by Jesus in Matthew 13 and 24.

Haggai Urged the Rebuilding of the Temple

Haggai returned with God's people after the exile. Along with Ezra the priest and prophet Zechariah, he worked on rebuilding the temple. He rebuked the people for their distractions of the Samaritans, and urged them to finish the temple rebuilding (Hag. 1). He foretold that God would *"shake all nations, so that the treasures of all nations shall come in, and I will fill this house with glory, says the Lord of hosts,"* (Hag. 2).

Zechariah Taught the Meaning of Worship

Zechariah means "whom Yahweh has remembered." Like his contemporary Haggai, he helped with the rebuilding of the temple, and encouraged its completion (Zech. 4). He urged the people to repent and of the consequences of God's judgment which had led them into captivity. He taught the people the meaning of worship (Zech. 8), and he foretold God's victory over all the earth (Zech. 14).

Malachi Announced John the Baptist and Christ

Malachi means "my messenger." The last book, set during Nehemiah, was followed by the 400 silent years before Christ. The temple was rebuilt, the city walls up, but the country was in drought and famine. The people were in doubt and spiritual lethargy, and he focused them on the duties of the priests, worship practices, and morality. Malachi closed the Old Testament with the announcement of John the Baptist and Christ: *"Behold, I send my messenger, and he will prepare the way before me. And the Lord whom you seek will suddenly come to his temple; and the messenger of the covenant in whom you delight, behold, he is coming, says the Lord of hosts,"* (Mal. 3:1).

CONSIDER how God used Isaiah and Malachi to present Christ's arrival, life, death and second coming. What comfort we have in knowing God's plans through the ages for giving us our Savior and Redeemer!

THE SAVIOR, SON OF GOD

MATTHEW

The four Gospel accounts—Matthew, Mark, Luke and John—give four perspectives on the same story and subject: the arrival and human walk on earth of the Messiah Son of God. (See Appendices V and VI, pages 256-257.)

Matthew's perspective especially witnesses to the Jewish audience, Mark's to the Romans, Luke's to the Greeks and Gentiles, and John's to the whole world. A key verse for Matthew is Peter's statement, *"You are the Christ, the Son of the living God,"* (Matt. 16:16).

QUESTIONS FOR PERSONAL THOUGHT AND DISCUSSION

1. Read Matt. 1—God Delivered Christ the King

a. List several ways God fulfilled *"what the Lord had said through the prophet,"* (Matt.1:22-23). (See also Isaiah 7:14).

b. How did the lineage of Christ help prove this?

c. Read Matt. 3:13-17. In what ways did Jesus' baptism help prove His identity?

2. Read Matt. 4:1-11—Satan's Test Proved Christ

What three things did Jesus tell Satan?

_____

_____

3. Scan Matt. 5-6—Christ Taught on a Mountain

a. What did Jesus see before He chose the mountainside?
    Why? (See Matt. 5:1.)

_____

b. Read the nine "blessed" characteristics, and God's promised
    blessings for each. (See 5:2-11.) What should be our
    response? (See verse 12.)

_____

_____

c. Read Matt. 6:6-13 and 7:7-12. Identify "praise, supplication,
    confession and protection" in Christ's model prayer. Why
    ask?

_____

_____

d. Read Matt. 6:25-34. List four things we are not to worry
    about.

_____

_____

4. Read Matt. 8:5-13—Easterners, Westerners, Sinners would Seek Christ; He Brings Peace

a. What was the basis for the Centurion's healing?

b. What did Jesus mean by those from the East and West? Who are subjects of the kingdom?

c. Read Matt. 9:9-13. Who were the Pharisees concerned about, and who did Jesus come with mercy to call?

5. Read Matt. 11:25-30—Jesus Is the Son of God

a. From whom were things hidden, and to whom were they revealed?

b. Describe the relationships of the Father, the Son, and the chosen.

c. Whose yoke are we to take? Why? Explain.

6. Scan Matt. 13—Christ Taught in Parables

Why did He use parables? (See verses 11-17.)

---

7. Read Matt. 14:15-33—Christ Performed Miracles

a. Why did Christ perform miracles? (See verses 31-32.)

---

b. Describe Peter's confession and his faith.

---

8. Read Matt. 22:37-40—Greatest Commandment

Describe the Greatest Commandment. (Compare Ex. 20:1-17.)

---

9. Scan Matt. 26-28, Read 27:32-54—Son of God

a. What names were discussed in verses 37, 40, 43, and 54?

---

b. Read 28:16-20. What names are important in our baptisms?

LESSON 16 SUMMARY

THE SAVIOR, SON OF GOD

MATTHEW

God Arrived as the Messiah, Son Jesus Christ

God completed His promise to all mankind of a Messiah with Christ, His Son. The first gospel in canon order by Matthew presented Christ as the Messiah, promised by God through the prophets over the course of time—from Abraham through Malachi—the *"Son of God."*

Jesus' genealogy, fulfillment of Old Testament prophesy, authority, and power are all emphasized by Matthew to prove His credentials as the Messiah. He was a master Teacher and Healer, unlike any before Him. In spite of His unique words and works, gradual mounting opposition culminated in His death on the cross. However, God's new King left an empty tomb, returned triumphant, and will again!

CONSIDER how Matthew was not only a Jew, but also a tax collector. He was chosen by God to tell the story of Christ to his Jewish brethren. He knew that all their kings had failed them! Now they cried once again for a new king. Matthew's goal was to show that Jesus was their promised eternal King, or "Messiah." He used Christ's quotes frequently from the Old Testament scriptures that foretold that he *"fulfilled what was written by prophets."* This is the basis for the "completion." Christ fulfilled the old law, rather than replace it. Consider how God's plan for your life redeems you to Himself through Christ.

Matthew Demonstrated Proof Christ Was Messiah

Matthew began by proving Jesus was the Messiah. Jesus was of the lineage of Abraham, Jesse and David, and the following generations to Joseph and Mary (Matt. 1). He confirmed who Christ's ancestors were and the facts surrounding His birth (Isa. 7, Matt. 2, Micah 5), just as the prophets had promised for centuries. Matthew not only appealed to the Jews by telling them things they had been taught, but also convinced many of God's gift—the fulfillment of His covenant.

Jesus was the Son of God. Even though He was conceived of God, He spent His entire human life defending His birth—that of God. This started with Satan's temptation (Matt. 4). With Peter, Andrew, James and John, He *"went throughout Galilee, teaching in their synagogues, proclaiming the good news of the kingdom, and healing every disease and sickness among the people,"* (Matt. 4:23). With this proof and defense, His fame spread throughout the land—as Gen.12:1-4 said!

Christ Spoke to the Crowds

Matthew then recorded Jesus' early ministry to the crowds of people as He delivered His gospel: how to be God's people; teach so all can hear; so all can talk to God; and so all can live righteously, leaving sin behind. Jesus did this in the mountainside sermon, starting with the "beatitudes," (Matt. 5-7). He stretched the minds of the hearers to go beyond the law—from unfelt actions to attitudes of the heart.

Then He led all of them to God in prayer with the "Lord's Prayer" (Matt. 6). In doing so, Jesus taught masses of people how to live with the law, how to talk to God, and how to live each day for their personal Lord. In concluding these sermons He taught the "Golden Rule" for Christian living and said, *"ask, seek and knock,"* (Matt. 7). Then, *"when Jesus had finished saying these things, the crowds were amazed at his teaching, because he taught as one who had authority, and not as their teachers of the law,"* (Matt. 7:28-29).

Christ proved He was the Son of God in the form of miracles that demonstrated His power to save men from sin and death. He cleansed the leper, healed the servant and Peter's mother-in-law, stilled the storm, cast out demons (Matt. 8), and healed the paralytic (Matt. 9).

Christ Selected His Apostles, Taught in Parables

He then called His 12 apostles (Matt. 10) and sent them first to the Jewish believers who hadn't yet accepted their Messiah. He instructed them that this was not a paid job—it was a "word of mouth," volunteer ministry that wouldn't be easy (Matt. 10-11).

Jesus, to His apostles and others, began a lecture series, teaching those that would listen in parables. *"Why?"* his disciples asked. He responded, *"Because the knowledge of the secrets of the kingdom of heaven has been given to you, but not to them,"* (Matt. 13, Isaiah 6).

God's leaders, as Isaiah had been, had received the Spirit in a way such to teach and understand the meaning behind His parables. He taught the parables of the sower, the wheat and the tares, the mustard seed, the leaven, the hidden treasure, the pearl, and the dragnet. He then asked about their understanding, *"'Have you understood all these things?' Jesus asked. 'Yes,' they replied,"* (Matt. 13:51).

Christ Taught With Miracles and Prophecies

Matthew recorded the death of John the Baptist (Matt. 14), followed by Jesus' miracles—feeding the five thousand, and walking on water demonstrating Peter's faith, lack of faith, and desire for faith (Matt. 14). Matthew then recorded the demonstration of Peter's faith in his confession, *"You are the Christ, the Son of the living God."* (Matt. 16:16).

He foretold to His disciples His death, resurrection and second coming (Matt. 16). In an act that demonstrated He was God, Jesus was transfigured as an angel of God, flanked by Moses and Elijah. With Him also were Peter, James and His brother John. He gave them, in strict confidence, a glimpse of Himself as God and then foretold again His death and resurrection (Matt. 17).

Preparing for their ability to understand the coming death and ultimate forgiveness for all sin, Christ gave a lesson on humility and forgiveness (Matt. 18). Once they understood sufficiently, Christ *"transferred the Kingdom"* in the final "triumphal entry" into Jerusalem (Matt. 21).

There was more work to be done in Jerusalem, with many more lessons to be learned. Jesus began with the cleansing of the temple (Matt. 21). He taught using more parables leading up to the "Greatest Commandment" (Matt. 22). They then asked questions about the Messiah, and He answered that He was indeed the Son of God.

Jesus harshly rebuked any distortions of His teaching—which He called the truth—with His "woes" to the Pharisees, *"Woe to you, teachers of the law and Pharisees, you hypocrites! You shut the door of the kingdom of heaven in people's faces. You yourselves do not enter, nor will you let those enter who are trying to,"* (Matt. 23:13).

Christ Proved Himself the King Eternal

Matthew recounted Jesus' betrayal and arrest, and Peter's denial of Jesus (Matt. 26). In the high court of Caiaphas, the high priest, Jesus was once again questioned on His birthright.

He asked Him if He was *"the Christ, the Son of the living God?"* Finally, after a great display of human pride, jealousy, and unbelief, the Son of God yielded up His Spirit in His death for all sin. Following that surrender—many believed, saying, *"Truly this was the Son of God!"*

CONSIDER how God completed His covenant promise to mankind of a Messiah with Christ, His only Son and Savior. Consider how He used Matthew to convince many Jews that Christ is the Messiah, and how He uses His Word and many believers to share Christ every day. Consider your own blessings of Christ, and how your Redeemer might bless others through you today!

THE SAVIOR, SON OF MAN

MARK

Christ was every bit as much the Son of Man as He was and is the Son of God—fully human and fully God. Mark, writing His gospel that would travel with the empire's soldiers to Rome, emphasized this by showing that Christ was the Savior who was a Servant Redeemer of man. Mark's gospel is summarized with the verse, *"For even the Son of Man did not come to be served, but to serve, and to give his life as a ransom for many,"* (Mark 10:45).

QUESTIONS FOR PERSONAL THOUGHT AND DISCUSSION

1. Read Mark 1:14-17 and Gal. 4:4-7—Christ Proclaimed the Gospel of Redemption

a. What two things does Jesus require in His gospel? (See 1:15.)

b. What does "fullness of time" mean? (See 1:15 and Gal. 4:5.)

c. In your own words, explain "redemption" and "fishers of men."

2. Read Mark 2:1-17—Jesus Healed and Forgave

a. Why do you think Christ healed with miracles before addressing sin? What was the outcome of those watching?

_____

_____

b. Why did Jesus spend time with sinners? (See 2:17.)

_____

_____

3. Read Mark 2:21-22—"Old Cloth, New Patch; Old Wineskin, New Wine" Illustrations Given

What did Christ mean by the "old and new" problems? (See also Rom. 12:2.)

_____

_____

4. Read Mark 2:23-27—Lord of the Sabbath

Explain what Christ meant about the purpose of the Sabbath.

_____

_____

5. Read Mark 6:1-13—Jesus' Hometown Disbelief

a. Why did Jesus' hometown friends reject Him?

_____

_____

b. How did the miracles and healings help their testimony?

_____

6. Read Mark 7:1-9—Traditions Rather Than God

a. What traditions were getting in the way of the Jews' belief in God?

_____

_____

b. How might traditions today distract us? Which ones?

_____

_____

7. Read Mark 7:14-23—Inward Defilement and Sin

a. What things defile a person? (See also Rom. 3:9-12, 21-26.)

_____

_____

b. What is our alternative and response?

_____

8. Read Mark 9:14-29—Belief and Unbelief

What did Jesus say is possible with belief? (See 9:23.) What else did Jesus say could make the miracle possible? (See 9:24, 29.)

---

9. Read Mark 12:41-44—The Widow's Mite

Did the largest sum or smallest sum have the most value? Explain.

---

10. Read Mark 13:32-37—The Day and the Hour

Who specifically knows exactly when Christ will come again? Why is this confidential? Explain.

LESSON 17 SUMMARY

THE SAVIOR, SON OF MAN

MARK

Christ is Fully God and Fully Man

Mark's account of Jesus' life on earth is that of the Servant who is constantly traveling to teach, heal, and finally die for the sins of His fellow man. That pattern of selfless service becomes the pattern also for those who will follow in the Servant's steps of Christian service.

Mark is the first written, shortest and simplest of the four gospels. It gives a crisp, moving account of Jesus' life. The narrative speaks for itself with Mark adding little of his own comments. The author Mark is the son of a church leader, Mary, who used her house as a meeting place for believers in Jerusalem (Acts 12). Peter must have gone to this house often because the servant girl recognized his voice at the gate. Peter was his close associate who may have led him to Christ. He called him *"Mark my son"* (1 Pet. 5), and it was this close association that gives Mark's gospel the authority of the apostles.

CONSIDER how God sent His Son for you—with all the power of Himself as the Son of God. But also consider how He came as your Servant—the Son of Man who forgives your inabilities and instead, works for and through you. Consider how your power is really Christ's righteousness working through you. What a great God would give you the power of a King and also do the works for you as your Servant, the Son of Man.

Mark may have been the *"certain young man"* at Gethsemane (Mark 14:51), which would make this book a first-hand account as by then all of the disciples had abandoned Jesus.

Barnabas was his cousin (Col. 4), and he and Paul took Mark along with them when they returned from Jerusalem to Antioch (Acts 12), and again on their first mission trip (Acts 13). Mark was with Paul when he wrote to the Colossians (Col. 4) and later Paul asked to see him (2 Tim. 4).

Christ is Man, a Servant and Teacher

Mark started his story of the Son of Man—the Servant—recalling the prophet Isaiah's promise of a *"messenger."* He continued with an introduction of Jesus by John, and then began the teaching-and-convincing dialogue with the temple and healing examples (Mark 1).

Mark gave examples of miraculous healings by the *"servant of man,"* when a paralytic was healed and forgiven (Mark 2). *"'But I want you to know that the Son of Man has authority on earth to forgive sins.' So he said to the man, 'I tell you, get up, take your mat and go home.' He got up, took his mat and walked out in full view of them all. This amazed everyone and they praised God, saying, "We have never seen anything like this!"'* (Mark 2:10-12).

The scribes and Pharisees couldn't understand the "new" practices being taught and demonstrated by Christ and His disciples.

They were waiting for their Messiah, but Jesus was telling them that He, their "bridegroom," was already here, and that there was a new message for them here. Christ used this parable to explain how the "new" related to the "old:" *"No one sews a patch of unshrunk cloth on an old garment. Otherwise, the new piece will pull away from the old, making the tear worse. And no one pours new wine into old wineskins. Otherwise, the wine will burst the skins, and both the wine and the wineskins will be ruined. No, they pour new wine into new wineskins,"* (Mark 2:21-22).

The Son of Man Brought a New Gospel

Those who would receive the new message must be like it—they also must be new. The new King wasn't challenging God's old commandments, but He was challenging man's use of them, such as the reasons for the Sabbath (Mark 2).

The Pharisees couldn't see beyond the letter of the law to learn the purposes of God. They couldn't see that the law was a means to an end—Christ's new offer of freedom and salvation from sin.

Proving He was both man and God, Jesus then focused them on His name—and His Spirit—the Holy Spirit. He said, *"Truly I tell you, people can be forgiven all their sins and every slander they utter, but whoever blasphemes against the Holy Spirit will never be forgiven; they are guilty of an eternal sin,"* (Mark 3:28-29).

He was summoned by His birth-mother and brothers, and He drew a comparison to His spiritual family (Mark 3:31-35). Jesus' earthly brothers and sisters are mentioned when He went back home to Nazareth, where He was treated not as their King but as a regular local sibling (Mark 6:1-8).

Jesus taught about the danger of ritual traditions and how they can become distractions, losing the spiritual meanings behind them (Mark 7:8-23).

After feeding four thousand people, the Pharisees wanted even more signs. Mark writes, *"The Pharisees came and began to argue with him, seeking from him a sign from heaven to test him. And he sighed deeply in his spirit and said, 'Why does this generation seek a sign? Truly, I say to you, no sign will be given to this generation. Truly, I say to you, no sign shall be given to this generation,'"* (Mark 8:11-12).

He cured a boy with evil spirits (Mark 9), and the father said, with pure faith, *"I believe; help my unbelief!"* This wasn't just about Jesus' miraculous ability—it was all about the father's humble confession of doubt, and ability to ask for a saving faith and belief in his Lord.

Christ Died and Returned to Save Sinners

After Jesus went to Judea and taught about marriage, blessed the little children, and told about the rich young ruler, He foretold Christ's death and resurrection to His apostles (Mark 10:32-45). Mark then wrote the summary passage of his book, *"For even the Son of Man did not come to be served, but to serve, and to give his life as a ransom for many,"* (Mark 10:45).

Jesus went to the temple to restore its use to God's intention by driving out the profiteering by those selling goods (Mark 11). The Jewish leaders feared Him because of His many followers, and His challenge of their practices of commerce in worship.

Jesus gave the great commandment (Mark 12) and asked the unanswerable question (also in Matt. 22). He warned the scribes about lengthy prayers and told about the widow's mite (Mark 12:41-44).

Jesus, a Healer and Servant of man—was indeed the Son of Man, as He called Himself. His purpose was to redeem us to His Father through His death. *"Afterward he appeared to the eleven themselves as they were reclining at table, and he rebuked them for their unbelief and hardness of heart, because they had not believed those who saw him after he had risen. And he said to them, 'Go into all the world and proclaim the gospel to the whole creation. Whoever believes and is baptized will be saved, but whoever does not believe will be condemned,'"* (Mark 16:14-16).

CONSIDER how God gave to mankind a human King in Christ, His Son—a Servant, Healer and Savior of man. Consider today where you are in your own personal relationship with your Creator, Light and Redeemer, Jesus Christ.

THE RISEN LORD IS OUR SAVIOR REDEEMER

LUKE

Luke wrote his account of the gospel of Jesus Christ especially for the Greeks—an educated, science-minded and philosophical audience. The Greek universities influenced all of the empire, making accurate, fact-based details especially important to Luke. As a highly educated doctor, he had the respect and abilities to be a credible and reliable spokesperson and historian for the new King of the Jews.

QUESTIONS FOR PERSONAL THOUGHT AND DISCUSSION

1. Read Luke 2:1-21—Christ Was Born to Mary

a. What was "normal" about Christ's birth?

b. What was miraculous and unusual about Christ's birth? (See also 1:26-38 and Isaiah 7:14.)

2. Read Luke 7:28-30—The Kingdom's Greatest

What do you think Jesus means in comparing John the Baptist to believers in His Kingdom?

3. Read Luke 7:36-50—Forgiveness Measured by Sins Forgiven, Love Given

How does forgiveness relate to love, and to being forgiven?

4. Read Luke 9:23-27, 57-62—Following Jesus

a. How are we to follow Jesus?

b. What is the cost of following Jesus?

5. Read Luke 11:33-35—The Light in You

Using this passage, if Christ is the Light of your life, how does your light shine to others?

_____

_____

6. Scan Luke 15—Prodigal Son and Lost Sheep

Compare the lost sheep to the prodigal son. Which son is more like the lost sheep? Which displays selfishness? (See 15:28-30.)

_____

_____

7. Read Luke 17:20-21—The Kingdom of God

Describe in your own words the Kingdom of God. When is it in effect?

_____

_____

8. Read Luke 22:14-20—The Lord's Supper

Describe the Last Supper and compare with your celebration of the Lord's Supper.

_____

_____

9. Read Luke 22:66-23:5—The Testimonies of the Council and Pilate

Upon whose testimony did the council depend for Christ's identity? Describe Pilate's judgment, and how he decided.

10. Read Luke 23:26-43—The Two Criminals at the Crucifixion

Which of the two criminals believed in the Christ? How did Jesus treat him?

11. Read Luke 24:1-12—Christ Is Resurrected

What was particular about the "third day"? (See also Luke 18:33.)

12. Read Luke 24:44-53—The Great Commission

Read also Acts 1:4-11. Briefly compare Luke's two accounts.

LESSON 18 SUMMARY

THE RISEN LORD IS OUR SAVIOR REDEEMER

LUKE

Luke Traced the Details of Christ's Life and Death

Luke, more than any other gospel, captured in detail the "major life events" of Jesus' life, death and resurrection—rising up from death as our Savior Redeemer. Luke wrote his accounts later than Mark (who wrote first) and Matthew (second), and while he was not a personal acquaintance of Jesus, he interviewed many followers of Christ for his writings. He was thorough and thoughtful in his editing.

Luke was a Greek doctor. Besides the Jews and Romans, the Greeks were also preparing for Christ's coming. Luke was the only Gentile author in the New Testament, responding to the Great Commission to take the gospel everywhere, to everyone. A friend and companion of Paul, he continued his writing with the book of Acts. These two books give a complete "linear history" of the New Testament. Like a timeline, the other books' events can "fit in" chronologically to Luke and Acts as added details. One can add Revelation to continue the timeline with the future judgment of believers and the world.

CONSIDER how God used the four Gospel writers to give us a full picture of Christ. Consider how Jesus used so many witnesses, teachings and miracles to prove to the world His identity, in order to offer salvation upon belief.

Consider how you might witness to others Christ's teachings and blessings you have received, and how you are His light and blessing to the world around you.

Christ's Birth, Youth and Ancestry

Luke's first chapter captured the angel's prophesy and fulfillment of John the Baptist's birth—the "messenger" (Mal. 3:1)—who came preparing the people for the Lord Jesus Christ. This theme is the same as that of the whole Old Testament—making the earth's peoples prepared and ready to meet their Lord.

Luke said, *"and he will go before him in the spirit and power of Elijah, to turn the hearts of the fathers to the children, and the disobedient to the wisdom of the just, to make ready for the Lord a people prepared,"* (Luke 1:17).

Luke then told the "Christmas Gospel" including the story of the angel Gabriel's foretelling of Christ's birth (Luke 1) and childhood (Luke 2). From a miraculous virgin birth to a relatively "normal" childhood, Jesus was and is both the Son of God and the Son of Man.

Mary and Joseph presented their child Jesus at the Temple in Jerusalem to the Priest Simeon. He blessed the child, saying, *"my eyes have seen your salvation that you have prepared in the presence of all peoples, a light for revelation to the Gentiles, and for glory to your people Israel,"* (Luke 2:30-32). Luke wrote in verse 52, *"And Jesus increased in wisdom and in stature and in favor with God and man."*

Luke cited John the Baptist's preparation for Christ with Isaiah's prophesy, *"As it is written in the book of the words of Isaiah the prophet, The voice of one crying in the wilderness: 'Prepare the way of the Lord, make his paths straight. Every valley shall be filled, and every mountain and hill shall be made low, and the crooked shall become straight, and the rough places shall become level ways, and all flesh shall see the salvation of God,'"* (Luke 3:4-6).

Mary's lineage is used in Luke's genealogy of Jesus (Luke 3), whereas Matthew used the proper Jewish legal lineage of Joseph (Matt. 1).

Christ Expanded Ministry and Faced Rejections

The next several chapters give accounts of Jesus' temptation by Satan (Luke 4), healings (Luke 4-9), and the calls of disciples and twelve apostles (Luke 5-9). Jesus had authority over every aspect of man's life—over demons, disease, nature, sin effects, and all people.

Jesus was teaching primarily about God's love and forgiveness for all. He ate with a Pharisee when a sinful woman came to Him and wept, and wiped His feet with her hair and tears. She anointed them with ointment. As Christ forgave all her many sins, He illustrated to the Pharisees that *"forgiven much, she loved much,"* (Luke 7). Christ showed them that her forgiveness had less to do with her sins than with her abundance of love toward Him.

Following are Jesus' parables, His miracles of stopping the storm on the sea, of casting out demons (Luke 8), of feeding five thousand people, His receiving of Peter's confession, and His foretelling to the apostles His death and resurrection (Luke 9). He then commissioned them to *"go and proclaim the kingdom of God,"* (Luke 9:60). Jesus sent out 72 evangelists to heal the sick and say, *"The kingdom of God has come near to you,"* (Luke 10).

These chapters illustrate dual responses to Jesus' teachings and miracles—belief with many following Him, and disbelief with many rejecting Him. From that time forward the intensity of opposition toward Christ increased. Jesus gave methods for personal evangelism to His disciples (Luke 10:1-12). Then He illustrated this new evangelism with the act of the good Samaritan (Luke 10:25-37). Jesus warned against seeking signs for physical desires (Luke 11), and He addressed the relationship of material possessions to one's heart, warning that He will come again unexpectedly (Luke 12).

Jesus told three parables of God's grace, starting with the story of the prodigal sons (Luke 15). Both sons were really lost, or "prodigal," in different ways. One was found—physically and spiritually, while the other jealously questioned the father's forgiveness of his brother. The rich young ruler story (Luke 18) puts into priority man's power and possessions. Another parable was about Zacchaeus, the wealthy, sinful tax collector, who repented and was converted (Luke 19).

Christ's Crucifixion and Victorious Resurrection

Jesus' triumphal entry into Jerusalem (Luke 19) led to the second cleansing of the temple. Jesus knew that He was on His last journey to Jerusalem. After entering Jerusalem, He encountered the opposition of the Jewish priests, Sadducees and scribes, and predicted the overthrow of Jerusalem. He instructed His disciples in the "Olivet Discourse" on several practical matters (Luke 21) including prayer, covetousness, faith, repentance, humility, evangelism, money, forgiveness, service, thankfulness, and salvation. He foretold the destruction of Jerusalem and His second coming. The last supper was the final Passover celebration with Jesus (Luke 22).

He instructed His disciples for a final time before Judas' betrayal in Gethsemane, and before Peter's denial of Him as the Christ. Luke 22:34 reads, *"He said, 'I tell you, Peter, the cock will not crow this day, until you three times deny that you know me.'"*

Jesus went before the Jewish Sanhedrin Council (Luke 22) where the High Priest Caiaphas charged Him with blasphemy but couldn't sentence death. The Council sent Him to Pontius Pilate who found Him innocent but of another jurisdiction. Pilate then sent Jesus to be tried by Herod who was the Roman-appointed governor and judge over Galilee (Luke 23:1-5). Herod found Jesus in contempt, but simply returned Him to Pilate, who found Him innocent (Luke 23:6-16). Pilate ultimately relented to the Jews' pleas for His death (Luke 23:18-49).

The resurrection of Jesus (Luke 24) contains the glory and foundation of the Christian message. The Lord conquered the grave—and death itself—as He had promised. He then appeared in proof of His bodily resurrection on a number of occasions to His disciples before His ascension to be with the Father.

CONSIDER how Christ's resurrection is a foreshadowing of your own resurrection offer entering eternal life with your Creator, Light and Redeemer. Praises for His everlasting mercy and grace!

SALVATION IS FOR BELIEVERS

JOHN

Whereas Matthew wrote especially to the Jews, Mark to the Romans, and Luke to the Greeks and all Gentiles, John reflected on why Christ came—for the whole world to hear! Matthew, Mark and Luke are referred to as the "synoptic" or "parallel" gospels, and gave complementary accounts of the life on earth of Christ. John, on the other hand, explained the person of the Divine Christ, His oneship with the Father God, and the successive roles of the Holy Spirit.

QUESTIONS FOR PERSONAL THOUGHT AND DISCUSSION

1. Read John 1:1-18— The Word Became Flesh

a. What meanings might "Word" have?

b. How did the Word become flesh?

c. Compare 1:1-3 to Heb. 13:8 and Rev. 1:8, 22:13.

2. Read John 3:1-8—Born Again of Water, Spirit

a. In your own words, compare physical birth to spiritual rebirth.

_____

_____

b. Read 1 Pet. 1:3, 23. Compare Peter's and John's descriptions.

_____

_____

3. Read John 3:16-21—God So Loved the World

a. What is the result of God's love for His world?

_____

_____

b. Who will be saved? Who will come into the light? Compare also 2 Pet. 3:9.

_____

4. Read John 4:31-38— One Sows, Another Reaps

What are the gospel roles of the sower and reaper?

_____

5. Read John 5:37-47—Searching the Scriptures

a. What are some of the reasons the Jews did not believe Jesus?

_____

_____

b. What is the purpose Jesus gives for the Scriptures?

_____

6. Read John 6:26-40—I Am the Bread of Life

What is the "food that endures to eternal life"? What is the will of God, according to verse 40?

_____

7. Read John 10:1-9 and 14:1-7—The Good Shepherd's Door; The Way, Truth and Life

Compare the door (or gate) to the "way" to the Father. What is the only way to the Father?

_____

_____

8. Read John 11:17-27—The Resurrection and Life

Compare Lazarus' resurrection with Jesus' promises.

_____

_____

9. Read John 14:15-26 and 16:4-15—Jesus Promised to Send the Holy Spirit

a. What are some of the roles of the Holy Spirit?

b. When did Jesus send the Holy Spirit for His believers?

10. Read John 15:12-19—Jesus Chose His Own

According to verse 16, who chooses servants of God?

11. Read John 19:38-42, 20:1-29—Burial, Resurrection and Empty Tomb: Christ Is Alive!

a. Who brought Jesus for burial? (See also 3:1-15.)

b. Which two disciples ran to the tomb? Who was fastest? Who stated his confession of belief?

c. How did Jesus prove Himself to Mary? To Thomas?

LESSON 19 SUMMARY

SALVATION IS FOR BELIEVERS

JOHN

In Him Was Life Created—the Light of Men

John, the last gospel sequentially and the last written, draws mainly on explanations, discussions and events not found in the other gospels. John proves to his readers that Jesus is God, flesh, the Word for the earth's people, and a sacrifice for believers to have life in His name.

John's three letters and Revelation were written after this gospel, dating it around 70-90 A.D. (See Appendix VI, page 257.) This makes John one of the last surviving eyewitnesses of the Lord. This gospel has the clearest purpose stated of any in the Bible, *"these are written that you may believe that Jesus is the Christ, the Son of God, and that believing you may have life in his name,"* (John 20:31).

John's key word is *"believe,"* which requires both knowledge, *"you will know the truth, and the truth will make you free,"* (John 8:32) and response, *"to all…who believed in his name, he gave power to become children of God,"* (John 1:12). Therefore, if you want to understand the meaning of life, and receive grace to have it eternally, you will find in John's gospel these truths most directly from Jesus Christ.

CONSIDER how God gave Christ's Light as salvation for believers to have Life in His name. As we walk in His Light we shine His blessings as promised through Abraham, the patriarchs and the prophets. Consider how the Old Covenant promised that we receive God's blessings and then give them to others as a blessing. Consider daily to whom you might pass a blessing of Christ in the name of your Christ Redeemer and Savior.

Christ Was Here From the Beginning

Like no other Bible writer, John gives us the "big picture" of the Creator God's purpose and relationship to the Son's Light and Word for the world. *"In the beginning was the Word, and the Word was with God, and the Word was God. He was in the beginning with God. All things were made through him, and without him was not any thing made that was made. In him was life, and the life was the light of men. The light shines in the darkness, and the darkness has not overcome it."… "But to all who did receive him, who believed in his name, he gave the right to become children of God, who were born, not of blood nor of the will of the flesh nor of the will of man, but of God. And the Word became flesh and dwelt among us, and we have seen his glory, glory as of the only Son from the Father, full of grace and truth,"* (John 1:1-5, 12-14).

The Word, Jesus Christ, is God's mouthpiece for His created. The Son of God became man—and is for us the Son of Man. In this divine combination we can relate with and learn from God (2 Tim. 3:16).

Jesus explained being *"born again"* while teaching Nicodemus (John 3). Jesus told him, *"Truly, truly, I say to you, unless one is born again he cannot see the kingdom of God."* (John 3:3). Jesus continued, *"that whoever believes in him may have eternal life. For God so loved the world, that he gave his only Son, that whoever believes in him should not perish but have eternal life. For God did not send his Son into the world to condemn the world, but in order that the world might be saved through him,"* (John 3:15-17). This dialogue helps to clarify and explain the purpose of life itself.

Jesus later met the Samaritan woman at the well and told her all that she ever did (John 4). And so, she told others, *"Come, see a man who told me all that I ever did. Can this be the Christ?"* John summarized this saying, *"Many Samaritans from that city believed in him because of the woman's testimony, 'He told me all that I ever did.'"*

He asked them to reap what has already been sown (John 4). When his disciples asked Him to eat, He said His food was *"to do the will"* of His Father, by His authority (John 5). After feeding over 5,000 people (John 6) with five loaves of bread and two fish, Jesus dealt with the peoples' desires for signs and temporal sustenance. He walked on water to get their attention.

Christ Describes Himself with the *"I Am"* Series

John recorded a series of Jesus' *"I Am"* self-identifying statements. The first was, *"I am the bread of life; whoever comes to me shall not hunger, and whoever believes in me shall never thirst."* (John 6:22-35).

In the second, Jesus said, *"I am the light of the world; he who follows me will not walk in darkness, but will have the light of life"* (John 8:12). The Pharisees argued His authority for such a statement, and Jesus clarified His relation to God, and their lack thereof. He said *"I am the Door, I came that they might have life; and I am the Good Shepherd"* (John 10:1-12). He then said, *"'I and the Father are one,' and the Jews took up stones again to stone him,"* (John 10:30).

Before raising Lazarus from the dead, He prophesied, *"I am the resurrection and the life"* (John 11). When Jesus had entered Jerusalem, He told them that the hour had come for the Son of Man to be glorified (John 12), and that *"Some love to praise men more than God."*

Jesus gave the people a view of the heaven where He was going and would prepare for them places. He described his Father's house *"with many rooms,"* and told them to believe as the way to find it (John 14). *"Thomas said to him, 'Lord, we do not know where you are going. How can we know the way?' Jesus said to him, 'I am the way, and the truth, and the life. No one comes to the Father except through me.'... 'Do you not believe that I am in the Father and the Father is in me? The words that I say to you I do not speak on my own authority, but the Father who dwells in me does his works,'"* (John 14:5-6, 10).

Jesus promised the Holy Spirit to His disciples and He offered to pray on each person's behalf to the Father (John 14). Each would receive the Holy Spirit as their Helper, as the Spirit is constantly with each believer, and is convicting the world of sin, righteousness, and judgment (John 14-17).

Jesus said, *"I am the true vine,...If you abide in me, and my words abide in you, ask whatever you wish, and it will be done for you,"* (John 15). He added, *"You did not choose me, but I chose you and appointed you that you should go and bear fruit and that your fruit should abide, so that whatever you ask the Father in my name, he may give it to you."*

Jesus' final days on earth were a combination of proving His identity, and fulfilling prophesies of His death and resurrection. As He was arrested He said, *"'Whom do you seek?' They answered him, 'Jesus of Nazareth.' Jesus said to them, 'I am he.'"* (John 18:4-5).

The Crucified Christ Lives and Saves!

After Peter denied Christ, they brought Jesus to Pilate at the governor's headquarters. *"Pilate said to him, 'So you are a king?' Jesus answered, 'You say that I am a king.'...Pilate said to him, 'What is truth?' After he had said this, he went back outside to the Jews and told them, 'I find no guilt in him.'"* Following this testimony and judgment, Pilate sought to release Him back to the Jews. They demanded that He be crucified (John 19). He died and was buried in a tomb authorized by Pilate.

The risen Jesus appeared first to Mary Magdalene and then to the disciples in Jerusalem. A few days later, Thomas was with them all when Jesus said, *"'Put your finger here, and see my hands; and put out your hand, and place it in my side. Do not disbelieve, but believe.' Thomas answered him, 'My Lord and my God!'"* (John 20:27-28).

CONSIDER how God used unbelievers, doubters and believers all to prove the Christ's identity. Consider the wonderful news to many of the Redeemer's resurrection!

EVANGELISM

ACTS

Acts records the beginning of the fulfillment of the Great Commission as announced by Christ in Matthew, Mark, Luke and John. The Old Covenant with Israel alludes to the Great Commission as God's people will be *"blessed to be a blessing to the whole world."* Acts traces the Spirit outpouring at Pentecost and the start and growth of the church. The gospel spread with the apostles' evangelistic mission trips, planting churches from Jerusalem, to Samaria and Judea, and to all the ends of the earth. (See Appendix VI, page 257.)

QUESTIONS FOR PERSONAL THOUGHT AND DISCUSSION

1. Read Acts 1:6-11—Commission and Ascension

a. When and with what power would they be Christ's witnesses? (See also Luke 24:44-52.)

b. Where will they be Christ's witnesses?

c. What occurred immediately following His statement? (See also John 7:37-39 and 16:7-15.)

2. Read Acts 2:1-12—The Gospel to Jerusalem

a. From what nations and languages were the devout Jews in Jerusalem? (Compare Gen. 11:1-9 and Josh. 24:14-15.)

b. In Peter's sermon, name a gospel prophesy of Joel and a couple of David's. (See 2:14-31.)

c. Name three or four points of Jesus' gospel. (See 2:32-41.)

3. Read Acts 3:18-26—Gospel Fulfilled Covenant

a. Describe how Christ's gospel fulfills the covenant. (See also Gen. 12:1-3.)

b. How might we be blessed by Christ's gospel? (See 3:26 and Rom. 3:21-26.)

4. Read Acts 6:7-15, 7:54-8:2—Stephen's Stoning

Who approved of Steven's execution, and what movement was occurring in Jerusalem?

5. Read Acts 9:1-9—Saul Sees the Light of Christ

a. Describe the confrontation and conversation between Saul and Jesus.

b. Read 9:10-19. Who was Ananias? How did Jesus describe Saul's new role in verses 15 and 28?

6. Read Acts 10:9-17, 30-43—Peter's Vision for Taking the Gospel to the Gentiles

Describe Peter's vision (10:9-17) and its meaning (44-48).

7. Read Acts 14:1-7—Paul's First Trip to Galatia

a. Where in the cities did Paul and Barnabas preach?

b. What were the reactions of Jews, Greeks, believers and unbelievers?

c. Read 14:8-19. What did Paul look for in the man? (See verse 9.) What was the Gentiles' reaction? The Jews'?

8. Scan Acts 16:1-5—Paul's Second Mission Trip

a. Who was Timothy? (See 16:1-5.)

b. Who was Lydia? (16:11-15.)

c. Where were Paul and Silas? Describe the Philippian jailer and his conversion. (See 16:22-36.)

9. Read Acts 19:21-29—Paul's Third Mission Trip

a. Describe the handmade gods in Ephesus, and the problem.

b. Read 20:22-24. What did the Holy Spirit tell Paul was ahead for him?

c. Summarize Paul's self-defense. (See 24:10-21.)

d. Read 28:17-31. Summarize Paul's last two years in Rome.

LESSON 20 SUMMARY

EVANGELISM

ACTS

The Church Was Blessed to be the World's Blessing

The events in Acts begin the fulfillment of the Great Commission as announced by Christ in the Gospels. The Old Covenant with Israel alludes to the Great Commission as God's people are *"blessed to be a blessing to the whole world."*

Acts traces the Spirit outpouring at Pentecost (Acts 2) and the start and growth of the church. The gospel spread with the apostles' evangelistic mission trips, planting churches from Jerusalem, to Samaria and Judea, and to all the ends of the earth. Luke continued the story from the end of the book of Luke, to John's Revelation to the seven churches.

Peter, the preacher, and John, the writer, were Christ's first apostles in Acts. Saul became Paul at his conversion (Acts 9), and was a transformed, born-again apostle and Christian. The other apostles were only mentioned in Luke's introduction, making the "Acts of the Apostles" a title relative to these. Traveling with Paul, the writer Luke was the principle eyewitness for the early development of the church.

CONSIDER how God first called Abraham, all of Israel, and His prophets and apostles. Consider His promise to share the blessings of His people to the ends of the earth. Like Paul, can we recognize the Christ who has offered Himself as our Savior Redeemer, and share with someone the good news of His gospel?

The Holy Spirit Took the Gospel to Jerusalem

The church's witness in Jerusalem (Acts 1-7) instructed when, who, where, how, and why God enacted the Great Commission, completing the Covenant with Abraham. Acts began with Luke's account of Christ's ascension, when Christ's disciples asked Him these same questions. *"They asked him, 'Lord, will you at this time restore the kingdom to Israel?' He said to them, 'It is not for you to know times or seasons that the Father has fixed by his own authority. But you will receive power when the Holy Spirit has come upon you, and you will be my witnesses in Jerusalem and in all Judea and Samaria, and to the end of the earth,'"* (Acts 1:6-8).

Christ made clear His selection of the timing. At the Feast of Pentecost, Jerusalem was filled with Jews visiting for the festival. The disciples were transformed with the Holy Spirit and excitement to proclaim the new message. In the Pentecost sermon (Acts 2) Peter proclaimed Christ and the baptism of the Spirit, *"'And in the last days it shall be, God declares, that I will pour out my Spirit on all flesh,'... 'And it shall come to pass that everyone who calls upon the name of the Lord shall be saved,'"* (Acts 2:17, 21). Three thousand believed, repented, were baptized, and forgiven of their sins. They received salvation as the gift of the Holy Spirit (Acts 2:41-47). In Peter's second sermon, he emphasized the fulfilled covenant with Abraham. He said, *"You are the sons of the prophets and of the covenant that God made with your fathers, saying to Abraham, 'And in your offspring shall all the families of the earth be blessed.'"* (Acts 3:25, Gen. 12:1-3).

The Apostles Were Empowered with Miracles

Peter and John continued their teaching (Acts 4) proclaiming Jesus' resurrection. Peter performed many miracles as illustrations of the authority of the Holy Spirit. These actions demonstrated the source and effectiveness of Christian power.

The Sadducees were annoyed at their claims and arrested them. Peter, filled with the Holy Spirit, told them, *"by the name of Jesus Christ of Nazareth, whom you crucified, whom God raised from the dead,"* and, *"for there is no other name under heaven given among men by which we must be saved,"* (Acts 4).

Luke continued his writing, giving historical accounts of church discipline with Ananias and Sapphira (Acts 5), the first deacons (Acts 6), growing opposition toward the church, early persecution, and Stephen's witness and public death by stoning in front of Saul, an appointed official of the Pharisee chief priests (Acts 7).

The Church Expanded To Judea and Samaria

The gospel was witnessed to the Samaritans in Judea (Acts 8-12), with Philip ministering at Samaria, giving healing signs and blessings, and converting Simon the magician and an Ethiopian eunuch (Acts 8).

Saul saw the Light of Jesus (Acts 9), and was converted on the road to Damascus becoming the born-again Apostle Paul. From that first day Paul was filled with the Spirit and preached boldly in the name of the Lord. The church was built up and *"in the comfort of the Holy Spirit, it multiplied,"* (Acts 9).

Peter continued his ministry with healings and the raising of Tabitha from the dead (Acts 9), converted Cornelius, and had the vision of the global mission to the Gentiles and every nation (Acts 10). He said, *"Truly I perceive that God shows no partiality, but in every nation any one who fears him and does what is right is acceptable to him,"* (Acts 10:34). Peter further defended Gentile evangelism, using the language of his vision, *"what God has cleansed you must not call common,"* (Acts 11).

Barnabas ministered at the Antioch church for a year. Antioch believers were the first to be called *"Christians"* (Acts 11). James was killed by King Herod in a martyr's death (Acts 12), and Peter, also under arrest, was released miraculously in an appearance of Christ. Even as the church faced growing persecution, it continued to increase in numbers throughout the Roman Empire.

The Church Expanded To the Ends of the Earth

The young church would witness to all the ends of the Earth (Acts 13-28). On Paul's first mission trip (Acts 13-14), he spread the gospel beyond Samaria to the Gentiles. Antioch, in Syria, gradually replaced Jerusalem as the headquarters of the church, and also became home base for all of Paul's mission trips. The Word of the gospel went out to the Galatian cities. Following this trip, a conference was organized in Jerusalem for the church's apostles and elders to discuss circumcision. They settled the disputed views between Jewish legal compliance and salvation by grace through faith alone (Acts 15:8-11, Gal. 2).

On the second mission trip (Acts 15-18) Paul returned to the Galatian churches and went on to Macedonia and Greece. Joined by Timothy, he stayed longest in Philippi, taught and baptized many. These included Lydia, a merchant of upscale apparel, and the jailer with whom Paul shared Christ's gospel just before the earthquake released all the prisoners. The jailer asked, *"what must I do to be saved?"* *"Believe in the Lord Jesus, and you will be saved,"* (Acts 16). Paul taught in Thessalonica, Berea, and Athens where he found the alter to *"the unknown god."* He said that God *"does not live in temples made by man,"* (Acts 17). After Corinth (Acts 18) he returned to Antioch.

On the third mission trip (Acts 18-21) Paul spent almost three years in Ephesus where he preached, *"it is more blessed to give than to receive,"* (Acts 20). Then he went on to Macedonia and Greece. When he returned to Jerusalem he was falsely accused of bringing Gentiles into the Temple. He was arrested and imprisoned. At his trial he said *"I have lived before God in all good conscience up to this day,"* (Acts 23). He was held prisoner for two years with no charges. Festus took the case to King Agrippa (Acts 26). Paul asked the King the question that led to his imprisonment in Rome: *"Why is it thought incredible by any of you that God raises the dead?"* (Acts 26:8).

CONSIDER how God promised Light for the world, and how He kept that promise with the Redeemer's gospel spread by millions of believers to the ends of the earth!

JUSTIFICATION

ROMANS

Romans traces the gospel of salvation—from condemnation (Rom. 3) to justification (Rom. 3-5), to sanctification (Rom. 6), to glorification (Rom. 8). It explains God's plan for Jews and Gentiles (Rom. 10-11), and concludes with practical advice for righteous living among believers (Rom. 12-16). Romans is both a book of theology—the study of God—and a study of practical exhortation and applications. The message is the good news of Jesus Christ.

QUESTIONS FOR PERSONAL THOUGHT AND DISCUSSION

1. Read Rom. 1:14-17—The Power That Brings Salvation to Believers; Righteous Live by Faith

In your own words, describe the gospel.

2. Scan Rom. 1:18-32—The Sinfulness of Mankind

What are some examples of sin and wickedness of mankind?

3. Read Rom. 3:9-20—No One is Righteous

a. Who is "naturally" righteous? (See 3:9-18.)

b. Who can be declared righteous by following God's laws?
(See 3:19-20 and 1 Tim. 1:8-11.)

4. Read Rom. 3:21-26—The Righteousness of God

a. How is the righteousness of God given? To whom?

b. How are we justified? (See verse 23.)

c. How is the atonement sacrifice to be received? (See verse 25.)

d. Why did He do this? (See verse 25b-26.)

e. How do we become conscious of our sins? (See verse 20.)

5. Read Rom. 5:1-5—Faith, Peace and Hope

Trace in these verses how we receive faith, peace, grace, hope, perseverance, and character.

6. Read Rom. 8:28-39—In All Things God Works for the Good of those Who Love Him

a. What does it mean to be called according to His purpose?

b. What is God's foreknowledge?

c. How does He predestine and conform us to Christ's image? (See also 2 Cor. 3:18.)

d. How does He justify?

e. How does He glorify?

f. Once justified, who can separate us from Christ? (See verses 31-39.)

7. Read Rom. 12:1-2 and 2 Cor. 3:16-18—Be Transformed

a. Using a dictionary define sanctification and transformation.

b. Compare Paul's words to the Romans and Corinthians.

8. Read Rom. 12:3-18, 15:1-7—Christian Service and Attributes

a. Describe how Christians with different functions and gifts are to serve together. (See 12:3-8.)

b. List about 15 attributes of Christians, as encouraged by Paul. (See 12:9-18.)

c. How might we encourage each other? (See 15:1-7.)

LESSON 21 SUMMARY

JUSTIFICATION

ROMANS

Justification is By Grace through Faith

To the Romans and people everywhere in all ages, Paul gives a systematic explanation of the gospel doctrine. It is both a book of theology—the study of God—and a study of practical applications.

The message is the good news of Jesus Christ. Salvation—the gift of God's justification removing sin. It requires belief, imputes righteousness, and is followed by a life of faith. Paul said, *"For I am not ashamed of the gospel, for it is the power of God for salvation to everyone who believes, to the Jew first and also to the Greek. For in it the righteousness of God is revealed from faith for faith, as it is written, 'The righteous shall live by faith,'"* (Rom. 1:16-17).

Paul explained, *"This righteousness is given through faith in Jesus Christ to all who believe. There is no difference between Jew and Gentile, for all have sinned and fall short of the glory of God, and all are justified freely by his grace through the redemption that came by Christ Jesus. God presented Christ as a sacrifice of atonement, through the shedding of his blood—to be received by faith,"* (Rom. 3:22-25).

CONSIDER how God recognizes the sinful nature in us, but instead of punishing us, He saves us from the sin itself! Consider His gift of His Son the Redeemer of our world.

> Consider how as sinners we know what we ought to do,
> but cannot do it. *"Who will rescue me from this body that
> is subject to death? Thanks be to God, who delivers me
> through Jesus Christ our Lord!"* (Rom. 7:24-25).

Since Paul did not found the church in Rome, it is likely that it began when some of the new Jewish believers returned from the Day of Pentecost (Acts 2). It is also likely that Christians moved to Rome from churches established by Paul in Asia, Macedonia and Greece. According to this letter, Gentiles were dominant in the Roman church.

The city of Rome had over a million people and was the largest and greatest in the world. The church was well known (Rom. 1:8) and long established. Paul wrote this letter from Corinth, Greece, in 57 A.D., near the end of his third mission trip (Acts 20).

Our Salvation Plan is God's Power through Faith

In this letter, Paul tried to build up this body of believers in Rome in their knowledge and faith, and to unite the Jews and Gentiles in working together as one church.

Paul's letter tracks the stages of man's salvation—from condemnation (everyone needs salvation), to justification (only Christ gives salvation), to sanctification (man's transformation), to glorification (in eternity). It turns mere truth to accountable, practical, righteous living.

Paul proved that the gospel is for everyone because everyone has sin. *"There is no one righteous, not even one;"* and *"no one will be declared righteous in God's sight by the works of the law; rather, through the law we become conscious of our sin,"* (Rom. 3). So Paul didn't void the law, but explained its place and role in the gospel. Christ's salvation completes and fulfills the law as we see our sin.

Paul said that those who have faith are justified by grace as a gift. Paul asked, *"Do we sin to receive grace?"* and answered his own question, *"By no means; we died to sin"* so it is dead (Rom. 6). Paul explained how faith is attained, saying *"I can will righteousness: but I cannot do it,"* (Rom. 7).

Paul said that as we receive Christ's righteousness, we have an obligation to live according to the Spirit in us. Once we receive righteousness, *"Therefore, there is now no condemnation for those who are in Christ Jesus, because through Christ Jesus the law of the Spirit who gives life has set you free from the law of sin and death,"* (Rom. 8:1-2).

Life and peace in Christ comes with a mindset of God's Holy Spirit—which we as believers will through our belief. *"Those who live according to the flesh have their minds set on what the flesh desires; but those who live in accordance with the Spirit have their minds set on what the Spirit desires. The mind governed by the flesh is death, but the mind governed by the Spirit is life and peace,"* (Rom. 8:5-6).

When we love Him, all things in our lives work toward His good. God's plan for believers and their faith has always been known to Him. He has always known those who would be called, justified, and glorified. *"And we know that in all things God works for the good of those who love him, who have been called according to his purpose. For those God foreknew he also predestined to be conformed to the image of his Son, that he might be the firstborn among many brothers and sisters. And those he predestined, he also called; those he called, he also justified; those he justified, he also glorified,"* (Rom. 8:28).

As He intercedes for us, no one can separate us from the love of Christ. *"We are more than conquerors through him,"* (Rom. 8:37).

Salvation Plan is for Jews and Gentiles

God's salvation plan is for Jews and Gentiles (Rom. 9-11). Paul clarified in this second section of Romans that God's apparent rejection of the Jews wasn't that at all. It was the Jews that rejected God—not God who rejected the Jews (Rom. 9).

Paul said that God's rejection was the fault of the Jews' lack of submission to God's righteousness (Rom. 10). *"Faith comes from what is heard, and what is heard comes by the preaching of Christ,"* (Rom. 10:17). Simply put, man cannot ever save himself. Salvation is God's mercy alone by Christ's work pursued through man's faith.

Paul said, *"If you declare with your mouth, 'Jesus is Lord,' and believe in your heart that God raised him from the dead, you will be saved. For it is with your heart that you believe and are justified, and it is with your mouth that you profess your faith and are saved,"* (Rom. 10:9-10).

We must Apply Our Salvation

God's righteousness is for our application (Rom. 12-16). In this final section, Paul shows that behavior must be built upon belief. These practical exhortations are necessary to enliven the salvation teachings of the first sections. Paul called us to be *"transformed by the renewing of your mind. Then you will be able to test and approve what God's will is—his good, pleasing and perfect will,"* (Rom. 12:1-2).

And to use diverse gifts, *"For just as each of us has one body with many members, and these members do not all have the same function, so in Christ we, though many, form one body, and each member belongs to all the others. We have different gifts, according to the grace given to each of us,"* (Rom. 12:4-6a).

He warned of personal conduct in relationships and community—that we must *"be subject to authority"* in our lives and work, and to work within the law (Rom. 13). *"Therefore let us stop passing judgment on one another. Instead, make up your mind not to put any stumbling block or obstacle in the way of a brother or sister,"* (Rom. 14:13). We must bear the failings of the weak (Rom. 15), and avoid dissensions in the church and those who speak against Christ's doctrine (Rom. 16).

CONSIDER how God establishes each believer's own righteousness in accordance with Christ's gospel, in keeping with His many promises. Consider how He wants all to come to an obedience that comes from faith! Praises to the only wise God and glory forever through Jesus Christ! Amen. (See Rom. 16:25-27.)

CHRISTIAN LOVE

1, 2 CORINTHIANS

The pagan and materialistic culture of Corinth at the time of Paul's letters demonstrates that the strong Christian church and fellowship can live in any culture where God puts it. This young Corinthian church, like many today, was a stark contrast to its sin-bound surroundings. But as a church, its members were committed by Jesus' Great Commission (Luke 24) to be a blessing to the world (Gen.12). In these letters Paul spoke to their personal and community challenges.

QUESTIONS FOR PERSONAL THOUGHT AND DISCUSSION

1. Read 1 Cor. 1:10-17—Church Factions

a. Describe the nature of the church divisions.

b. According to Paul, who are we to follow as Christians?

2. Read 1 Cor. 1:18-31—Godly Wisdom vs Man's

a. In your own words, how would you describe "the word of the cross"? (See verses 18, 27-30.)

_____

_____

b. In Paul's day, what did the Jews seek? The Greeks? (See verse 22.) What did Paul preach to them?

_____

_____

3. Read 1 Cor. 8:1-13—Liberty a Stumbling Block

a. How could liberty for one Christian be a stumbling block for another? (See verses 9 and 12.)

_____

_____

b. Explain Paul's example of forbidden foods and idolatry.

_____

_____

c. Name one or two "stumbling blocks" that you may need to consider in your Christian liberties.

_____

_____

4. Read 1 Cor. 10:12-13—No Temptation Too Great

a. Is anyone strong enough to avoid temptation?

b. Does God ever allow us to be tempted beyond our ability to escape and/or endure it?

c. From where does temptation come? (See James 1:12-15.)

5. Read 1 Cor. 13:1-13—Love is Patient and Kind

a. What three attributes does Paul say are nothing without love? (See verses 1-3.)

b. What 15 attributes does Paul advise us to have that demonstrate Christian love? (See verses 4-7.)

c. What never ends? Why is that important?

d. What three things "abide"? Which is greatest?

6. Read 2 Cor. 3:1-6—Christ Makes Us Competent

In Christ, what recommendations do we need? Where do we get our confidence, competence and life?

7. Read 2 Cor. 3:7-18—Transformed By Degree

a. In these verses compare the ministry of Moses to the ministry of Christ.

b. How are we transformed with ever-increasing glory?

8. Read 2 Cor. 5:14-21—In Christ a New Creation

Describe the message of reconciliation. (See verse 19.)

9. Read 2 Cor. 9:6-14—God Loves a Cheerful Giver

Describe a cheerful giver. Where do we get the grace to be a cheerful giver? (See verse 14.)

LESSON 22 SUMMARY

CHRISTIAN LOVE

1, 2 CORINTHIANS

Paul Called the Church to Unity and Sanctity

This young Corinthian church, like many today, was a stark contrast to its sinful surroundings. But as a church, the Christian believers committed by Jesus' Great Commission to be a blessing to their world. Paul in these letters spoke to the challenges they faced as individuals, families and the body of Christ in Corinth and the world.

Paul's Corinthian letters illustrate the practical responses to the doctrines found in his earlier letter to the Romans. Key elements show that the difficulties facing these new Christians were the follies of seeking human wisdom and education over seeking God. The Corinthians faced human follies of pride in education and sexual impurity. He emphasizes the basis of their belief is not found in human wisdom, but in *"Christ crucified and the power of God."*

CONSIDER how God dealt first with evil in the Garden of Eden, and again on the Calvary cross. But also consider how He wants to deal daily with sin in our lives, and to protect us from the evil influences of the world around us. Consider the blessing and gift of God of the Redeemer Christ who took sins away. Praise Him for transforming our sinful self—degree by degree—into the likeness of Christ Himself! Consider what it means to be an image-bearer of the Living God!

The pagan and materialistic culture of Corinth at the time of this letter demonstrates that the strong Christian church fellowship can survive and thrive anywhere God puts it.

Corinth was a strategic commercial center. Its wealth and mixed cultures were reflected in pagan alters anywhere one looked—to Poseidon, Artemis, Hermes, Zeus, Apollo—and many other gods and goddesses. The temple of Aphrodite decorated a hill overlooking the city and encouraged religious immorality to its visitors.

The Corinthian Christians were influenced by these sinful and pagan worldviews continuously obvious from every direction. Paul in these letters spoke to their personal and community challenges to meet their needs as godly Christians and the church.

Paul Addressed Factions within the Church

Many members of the Corinthian church had become overly loyal to the leaders of this new church—above their loyalty to Jesus Christ. Paul wrote, *"For it has been reported to me by Chloe's people that there is quarreling among you, my brothers. What I mean is that each one of you says, 'I follow Paul,' or 'I follow Apollos,' or 'I follow Cephas,' or 'I follow Christ.' Is Christ divided? Was Paul crucified for you? Or were you baptized in the name of Paul?"* (1 Cor. 1:11). They had made idols of their leaders, losing focus of Christ's gospel. Paul warned of this danger and divisiveness.

Human Wisdom and Foolishness Abounded

Paul's focus on the folly of human "wisdom" and striving toward human knowledge reflecting Corinth's misunderstanding of education and philosophy (1 Cor. 1). God wants His people to be educated and have sharp intellect. But His wisdom and education are found in a godly attitude with the ability to live in His image, and encourage the same in others. This wisdom gives God's people the ability to achieve full potential in His image. Paul said that when the basis of the Christian view is *"Christ crucified and the power of God,"* then spiritual things are folly to the unspiritual (1 Cor. 2). Everything—the Spirit and judgment—is from God who gives judgment (1 Cor. 4).

Counsel on Family, Fellowship and Salvation

Paul's words to the Corinthians about human strengths and weaknesses reveal a misunderstanding by Corinth of what God's strength means and how He views the value of weakness. Paul counseled this young church on maintaining fellowship with immoral members (1 Cor. 5).

Sinful conduct had led to lawsuits among fellow believers (1 Cor. 6), so he counseled them on their steps to settlement and judgment. Paul gave Christ's views on marriage and divorce (1 Cor. 7). He focused his Corinthian readers on chastity and purity, saying, *" 'It is good for a man not to have sexual relations with a woman.' But because of the temptation to sexual immorality, each man should have his own wife and each woman her own husband,"* (1 Cor. 7:1-2).

Many thought that only the Spirit was inherently good, and the body was inherently bad. This was the Greek "gnostic" idea of a divided man—separated between body and soul. But Christ is clear that the body is the Lord's—both physical and spiritual. Therefore, Paul gives the high view of marriage and healthy sexual relationships (1 Cor. 7).

Christian liberty for some was becoming a stumbling block to others (1 Cor. 8). God will give us no temptation beyond our strength, Paul said, *"No temptation has overtaken you that is not common to man. God is faithful, and he will not let you be tempted beyond your ability, but with the temptation he will also provide the way of escape, that you may be able to endure it,"* (1 Cor. 10:13).

Spiritual gifts within the body of Christians differ with each member. Paul wrote, *"Now there are varieties of gifts, but the same Spirit; and there are varieties of service, but the same Lord; and there are varieties of activities, but it is the same God who empowers them all in everyone. To each is given the manifestation of the Spirit for the common good,"* (1 Cor. 12:4-7).

Paul Explains Sanctification, Being Transformed

Paul introduced the doctrine of sanctification to the Corinthians in his second letter. His themes were: the grace to grow (2 Cor. 1-4); the need to be born again (2 Cor. 3-5); and, the need to give (2 Cor. 8-9).

In one of the clearest understandings of the whole Bible regarding sanctification, Paul describes the process of being sanctified as that of being transformed—increasingly degree by degree—into the likeness of Christ. Paul said, *"But whenever anyone turns to the Lord, the veil is taken away. Now the Lord is the Spirit, and where the Spirit of the Lord is, there is freedom. And we all, who with unveiled faces contemplate the Lord's glory, are being transformed into his image with ever-increasing glory, which comes from the Lord, who is the Spirit,"* (2 Cor. 3:16-18).

Paul said that in Christ we are *"a new creation,"* (2 Cor. 5), and that in Christ's reconciliation of us we become the *"righteousness of God,"* (2 Cor. 5). Our repentant grief is godly, leading to salvation (2 Cor. 7). Paul describes the glorification of our own resurrection, saying, *"Since we have that same spirit of faith, we also believe and therefore speak, because we know that the one who raised the Lord Jesus from the dead will also raise us with Jesus and present us with you to himself. All this is for your benefit, so that the grace that is reaching more and more people may cause thanksgiving to overflow to the glory of God,"* (2 Cor. 4:14-15).

Paul wrote to them about stewardship and giving (2 Cor. 8-9). He finished his letter with the message that grace is sufficient. It is God's perfect power that is for our weakness (2 Cor. 12).

CONSIDER how Paul prayed for the Corinthians, *"For the sake of Christ, then, I am content with weaknesses, insults, hardships, persecutions, and calamities; for when I am weak, then I am strong,"* (2 Cor. 12:10). Praises for the humility the Redeemer teaches us through Paul's sincere and humble teachings!

By Grace Through Faith

Galatians and Ephesians

In Paul's letters to the Galatian and Ephesian churches, we see how God protects His people from selfish legalism, and directs them to a grace-granted life of faith, love, redemption and discipline. Paul admonished Jewish legalism and defended Christian liberties (Gal. 1-5); instructed love and justification by faith (Gal. 6-Eph. 3); and instructed confession, forgiveness, and discipline (Eph. 4-6).

QUESTIONS FOR PERSONAL THOUGHT AND DISCUSSION

1. Read Gal. 1:6-17—Deserting the Gospel

a. What did Paul mean by "deserting the gospel"?

b. Who were the Judaizers, and what was the context of this Judaism and legalism? (See 1:13-14 and also Phil. 3:2-3.)

c. What might be a similar example of legalism today?

2. Read Gal. 2:15-3:14, Eph. 2:4-10—Justification by Grace through Faith

a. How is a Christian justified for salvation?

_____

_____

b. What are "works of the law"? Give an example.

_____

c. How do we "live by faith"? (See 3:14.)

_____

3. Read Gal. 3:21-29, Eph. 2:14-16—All Are One

What does it mean to be "one in Christ"?

_____

_____

4. Read Gal. 4:4-9 and Eph. 1:3-14—In the Fullness of God's Timing

a. What does it mean to be "redeemed as adopted sons"?

_____

b. When did God choose us? How did He predestine us and why?

_____

5. Read Gal. 5:16-26—Fruits of the Spirit

a. What does it mean to walk by the Spirit? To be led by the Spirit? To live by the Spirit?

b. What are the fruits of the Spirit?

6. Read Gal. 6:1-10—Bear Another's Burdens

What does it mean to "bear another's burden" as a Christian?

7. Read Eph. 1:7-10, 19-23—God's Unity Plan

a. What does Paul mean that "all things will be united in Him"? (See also Eph. 2:13-16.)

b. What does it mean that He "put all things under His feet" and made Him head over the church body?

8. Read Eph. 4:1-7, 17-31—Unity and Gifts of the Body of Christ

a. Write seven things Paul describes as "one." (See 4:1-7.)

_____

_____

b. How does Paul describe the "old self"? (See 4:17-23.)

_____

_____

c. How does he describe the "new self"? (See 4:21-31.)

_____

_____

9. Read Eph. 6:10-18—The Armor of God

a. Why do we need protection?

_____

b. Name six protections and their purposes.

_____

_____

_____

LESSON 23 SUMMARY

BY GRACE THROUGH FAITH

GALATIANS AND EPHESIANS

Paul Taught the Galatians Faith with Liberties

In Paul's letters to the Galatian and Ephesian churches, we see how God in His mercy gives grace and liberty, but requires His image-bearers to live in a grace-granted life of faith, love, redemption and discipline.

Paul admonished to the Galatians their Jewish legalism and defended Christian liberties (Gal. 1-5). He instructed Christian love and justification by faith to both churches (Gal. 6-Eph. 3). To the Ephesians he taught confession, forgiveness, and discipline (Eph. 4-6).

Jewish legalists wanted these new Christians to revert to their religious human gospel of works by the "letter of the law." Paul's letter was prompted by the inroads made into the churches by the Judaizers— Jewish Christians that insisted that Gentile converts to the Christian faith should submit to Jewish legalisms such as circumcision and food rituals.

CONSIDER how Paul's letter to the Galatians shows God's divine grace in the liberties that He grants to Christians. The justification Paul outlines is that of Christ's death to sin that alone produces righteousness in Christians and gives freedoms in their walk with Jesus. Consider how a life in Christ not only takes away our sin, but imputes the righteousness of Christ in its place! How wonderful it is to experience the freedoms from the bondage of sin—along with the privileges and responsibilities of bearing the image of God and Christ!

They attacked Paul personally, saying he was not a true apostle, and not equal to the original twelve apostles whose authority and prestige they claimed. Paul's apostleship was from God. His conversion and Christian ministry show that he is not inferior in authority to the apostles in Jerusalem (Gal. 1-2).

Paul Clarified the Gospel is by Grace through Faith

Paul called out the hypocrisy and emphasized to these churches that Christ's gospel grants a certain liberty in Christ. He said, *"we know that a person is not justified by works of the law but through faith in Jesus Christ, so we also have believed in Christ Jesus, in order to be justified by faith in Christ and not by works of the law, because by works of the law no one will be justified,"* (Gal. 2:15).

Paul describes Christian faith, and how it produces righteousness in us by living in Christ's image. He said, *"the life I now live in the flesh I live by faith in the Son of God, who loved me and gave himself for me. I do not nullify the grace of God, for if righteousness were through the law, then Christ died for no purpose,"* (Gal. 2:20b-21).

Paul went on to compare the law to Christian salvation. He said, *"Now it is evident that no one is justified before God by the law, for "The righteous shall live by faith," … "Why then the law? It was added because of transgressions, until the offspring should come to whom the promise had been made, and it was put in place through angels by an intermediary. Now an intermediary implies more than one, but God is one. Is the law then contrary to the promises of God? Certainly not! For if a law had been given that could give life, then righteousness would indeed be by the law. But the Scripture imprisoned everything under sin, so that the promise by faith in Jesus Christ might be given to those who believe,"* (Gal. 3:11, 19-22).

Paul Compared the Law to Christian Faith

The law was never a means of justification. Abraham was justified by faith 430 years before the law, and we are his spiritual descendants, sons and heirs (Gal. 3:29-4:7). With Christ's death on the cross and God's gift of the Spirit (Gal. 4:6-7), we know that salvation is a gift by grace through faith, not achieved through works of the law.

All of this was done in God's perfect timing. Paul wrote, *"But when the fullness of time had come, God sent forth his Son, born of woman, born under the law, to redeem those who were under the law, so that we might receive adoption as sons,"* (Gal. 4:4-5).

Paul said we are no longer slaves, but sons and heirs. Christ's grace gives us freedom to live. *"For freedom Christ has set us free; stand firm therefore, and do not submit again to a yoke of slavery,"* Paul said (Gal. 5:1). He distinguished Christian liberty (Gal. 5-6) by naming the *"works of the flesh"* and the *"fruits of the Spirit,"* (Gal. 5:19-26). The freedom to which we are called is not license to sin. It is the freedom of sons and heirs that enables us to bear one another's burdens, love each other, and live lives of self control and purity (Gal. 6).

Paul's Ephesian Letter Emphasizes God's Grace

Ephesian Christians were in several churches in the province of Asia. Paul had worked with these churches on his third mission trip (Acts 19). His ultimate purpose is to unite—by grace through faith—all of creation in Christ (Eph. 1:9-10). He called them to Christian love, as was written again in the end of his Galatian letter.

Writing from a Roman prison, the letter is written in calm, deliberate words, free of criticism. Paul refers to *"the riches of his grace, which he lavished upon us, in all wisdom and insight making known to us the mystery of his will, according to his purpose, which he set forth in Christ as a plan for the fullness of time, to unite all things in him, things in heaven and things on earth,"* (Eph. 1:7-10).

Paul states clearly that by grace through faith are we saved, *"For by grace you have been saved through faith. And this is not your own doing; it is the gift of God, not a result of works,"* (Eph. 2:8-9a).

Paul Calls for Unity in Christ and in His Church

Paul focuses his readers on unifying around the person of Jesus Christ and the church—the household of God—with *"Christ at the cornerstone"* (Eph. 2:19-20). It is through the church that *"the manifold wisdom of God is made known,"* (Eph. 3:10). The church is the body of Christ, who is at its head (Eph. 4:11-16). All believers are members of His universal church body (Eph. 1:23, 4:25, 5:23, 30). Jesus Christ in the church glorifies God (Eph. 3:21).

The one divine purpose to which God draws all of His creation is demonstrated in the redemptive work of Christ, His Son, resurrected, and glorified. It is manifest in the church, the body of Christ, into which all—Jews and Gentiles—are drawn in unity and peace (Eph. 2). This is the revealed mystery of God's redemptive plan (Eph. 3).

Paul addressed husbands, wives, parents and children, masters (bosses) and slaves (workers). He instructs that we all have privileges and responsibilities alike to persevere our calling. *"There is one body and one Spirit—just as you were called to the one hope that belongs to your call—one Lord, one faith, one baptism, one God and Father of all, who is over all and through all and in all. But grace was given to each one of us according to the measure of Christ's gift,"* (Eph. 4:4-7).

Paul bases his practical exhortations to us and to all Christians by affirming relationship to each other, to the world, and in the family (Eph. 4:1-6:20). As image-bearers of God, we are to *"be imitators of God, as beloved children. And walk in love, as Christ loved us and gave himself up for us, a fragrant offering and sacrifice to God,"* (Eph. 5:1). This is how we are to behave in the fellowship of the church, and in relation to the world. The relation of Christ to the church is like that of a husband to his wife (Eph. 5:22-23).

CONSIDER how God calls His people from selfish legalistic religion, and directs them to a grace-granted life of redemption, faith, love, in the image of our God and Redeemer.

JOY IN KNOWING CHRIST

PHILIPPIANS AND COLOSSIANS

Paul's two letters from prison in Rome to the Philippians and the Colossians show a joyous Christian who had found Christ to be all sufficient. Paul voiced his Christ-centered philosophy as, *"For to me to live is Christ, and to die is gain,"* (Phil. 1:21).

The Colossians' letter is perhaps the most illustrative of Christ in the Bible, showing us Christ's supremacy in creation and redemption, and our need for submission—to the Creator and Sustainer of all things (Col 1:16-17).

QUESTIONS FOR PERSONAL THOUGHT AND DISCUSSION

1. Read Phil. 2:1-10—Equality Not to be Grasped

a. What did Paul mean by Christ being "equal with God," yet humbled through death?

b. What are the purposes and results of this hard-to-grasp "God with human form"? (See Phil. 1:10-11.)

2. Read Phil. 3:7-11—Becoming Like Christ

a. How does the "power of the resurrection" make us like Christ? (See also Rom. 6:5 and 1 Thess. 2:14-18).

_____

_____

b. What is the goal? (See Phil. 3:14-21.)

_____

_____

3. Read Phil. 4:4-9—Rejoice Always!

a. In what ways, according to Paul in verses 4-7, can we rejoice in the Lord?

_____

_____

b. What eight things in verses 8-9 are we to practice?

_____

_____

4. Read Phil. 4:11-13—I Can Do All Things

In what circumstances might we "do all things through Him"?

_____

5. Read Col. 1:15-20—The Image of Christ

a. Name 12 attributes of Christ, according to these verses.

_____

_____

_____

_____

_____

b. Which attribute do you find most important to you?

_____

6. Read Col. 2:6-15—Living Faith vs. Traditions

a. What were "empty traditions" that could threaten their faith?

_____

_____

b. What did Christ say about traditions? (See Mark 7:5-9.)

_____

_____

7. Read Col. 3:1-17—Put On Your New Self

a. What things are we to "put to death"? (See Col. 3:5-9.)

_____

_____

_____

b. What things are we to "put on"? (See Col. 3:10-17.)

_____

_____

_____

8. Read Col. 3:18-4:6—Relating With Others

How should Christians relate to others?

a. Wives / Husbands / Fathers / Mothers (Col. 3:18-21)

_____

b. Workers / Employees / Bosses / Employers (Col. 3:22-4:1)

_____

c. Christians toward non-Christians (Col. 4:2-5)

_____

_____

LESSON 24 SUMMARY

JOY IN KNOWING CHRIST

PHILIPPIANS AND COLOSSIANS

Paul Sent From Prison Words of Joy and Christ

Paul's letters to the Philippians and the Colossians show us a joyous Christian apostle who had found Christ to be all sufficient, even under the worst of circumstances as he wrote from a Roman prison. He sent affection and gratitude to the Philippians, and relayed a clear vision of Christ's image of supremacy to the Colossians (Col. 1).

Paul's ministry in Philippi, in the province of Macedonia, was one of the most thrilling of all Christian missions. He went there by the Lord's call on his second mission trip (Acts 16). Years later he returned to the area of Macedonia on his third mission trip (Acts 20) and again on his way back to Syria.

The letter to the Philippians reflects mutual affection with this church and confidence in their ministry (Phil. 1-2). They were subject to Judaizers' legalistic teaching, so Paul clarified the faith-alone gospel (Phil. 3). These were friends that had often helped Paul with their gifts (Phil. 4) and had not forgotten him later when he was in prison.

CONSIDER how God gives you joy in partaking in His mercy and grace, growing in Christ's love, and sharing the gospel. Paul's Christian-life philosophy was *"For to me to live is Christ, and to die is gain,"* (Phil. 1:21). When you face hardship, remember how he said, *"Rejoice in the Lord always; again I will say, rejoice. Let your reasonableness be known to everyone. The Lord is at hand; do not be anxious about anything, but in everything by prayer and supplication with thanksgiving let your requests be made known to God,"* (Phil. 4:4-6).

Paul Called the Philippians to Unity and Humility

Paul wrote this letter expressing his thanks for a financial gift from the Philippians while in prison in Rome most likely about 59-60 A.D. The letter is simple, direct, and overflowing with love and thanksgiving (Phil. 1). While personal and practical matters are stressed more than theological matters, they were urged to understand the gospel of grace. By allowing his time in jail as an opportunity to preach the gospel, God had shown Paul that in all things He works for good with those who are called by Him. This was Paul's source of joy.

Humility, perseverance and optimism are the marks of the Christian life (Phil. 2). In all circumstances the Philippians were to be glad and to rejoice with Paul. Paul explained the equal-but-mysterious relationship of God and Christ—Father and Son—as one not to be fully understood. But Christ died *"so that at the name of Jesus every knee should bow, in heaven and on earth and under the earth, and every tongue confess that Jesus Christ is Lord, to the glory of God the Father,"* (Phil. 2:10-11).

False Teachings of Legalism Threatened Divisions

Paul warned of perils to be watched for by the church—enemies of the gospel within the church (Phil. 3) and outside (Phil. 1:27, 28). These perils must be withstood and defeated. The dangers of self-seeking and pride could lead to harmful divisions (Phil. 2).

Perseverance, hope, unity, and thanksgiving are to be made known to God. Paul exhorted commendable practices, acknowledged Christ's abundance (Phil. 4:8-12), and attributed all gifts to God, saying, *"I can do all things through him who strengthens me,"* (Phil. 4:13).

Paul Showed the Colossians Christ's Supremacy

In his letter to the Colossians, Paul addressed a group he did not know personally, having to introduce himself (Col. 1:1-4, 2:1). Colossae was located in the Lycus valley in the province of Asia, about 100 miles from Ephesus. It had at one time been the most important city in the area, but had experienced decline.

Paul wrote the letter from prison in Rome (Col. 4:3, 18) around 59 to 61 A.D., about the same time as his letter to Philemon. Paul had corresponded with and discussed the three churches' progress with Epaphras, a church leader from that area who had come to see Paul (Col. 1:7-8; 4:12-13).

The Colossians' letter was written primarily to counteract erroneous and dangerous teaching. Paul wrote, *"See to it that no one takes you captive by philosophy and empty deceit, according to human tradition, according to the elemental spirits of the world, and not according to Christ. For in him the whole fullness of deity dwells bodily, and you have been filled in him, who is the head of all rule and authority,"* (Col. 2:8-10).

This teaching, called "Gnosticism," deprived Jesus Christ of His unique status as Son of God, and as our only Savior. It reduced Christ to one of a series of divine created beings descending from God. Paul feared that asceticism, magical rites, worship of other bodies (Col. 2:16-19), which are derived from gnostic dualism, would reduce Christianity to another "self-made religion" (Col. 2).

Paul dealt with this dangerous heresy by proclaiming the uniqueness and complete sufficiency of Jesus Christ. Paul proclaimed the only Savior of all, *"He is the image of the invisible God..."* (Col. 1:15).

The Colossians were instructed to reject any system that would belittle the person of Jesus Christ. He wrote, *"If then you have been raised with Christ, seek the things that are above, where Christ is, seated at the right hand of God. Set your minds on things that are above, not on things that are on earth. For you have died, and your life is hidden with Christ in God. When Christ who is your life appears, then you also will appear with him in glory,"* (Col. 3:1-4).

The Colossians must stand fast in the faith holding to the hope contained in the gospel. In this, they must reject fanciful teachings that have to do with festivals and asceticism (Col. 3).

Christ Raises Us to a New Life and Conduct

In Christ they have been raised to a newness of life, and in Him all grace and virtues are to be found. Paul wrote, *"Put on then, as God's chosen ones, holy and beloved, compassionate hearts, kindness, humility, meekness, and patience, bearing with one another and, if one has a complaint against another, forgiving each other; as the Lord has forgiven you, so you also must forgive. And above all these put on love, which binds everything together in perfect harmony. And let the peace of Christ rule in your hearts, to which indeed you were called in one body. And be thankful,"* (Col. 3:12-15).

Paul taught accountability for husbands and wives, slaves and workers (Col. 3:18-25). And he taught accountability to everyone in making the most of your time, saying, *"Walk in wisdom toward outsiders, making the best use of the time. Let your speech always be gracious, seasoned with salt, so that you may know how you ought to answer each person,"* (Col. 4:5-6).

Paul's desire and ministry was for a church and people of God that would be strong in fellowship and truth, living out Christ for the glory of God.

CONSIDER how easy it might be to have the wrong view of Christ if we don't keep our eyes on Him as the Son of God, Messiah Christ, our Creator, Light and Redeemer. Consider how God used Paul and the Colossians to warn us of false gospels that distort and confuse Christ's identity and saving grace. May we look for opportunities to share Paul's description of the Living Christ and His gospel of salvation for believers!

WAITING FOR CHRIST

1, 2 THESSALONIANS

Paul wrote to the Thessalonians these two letters commending them as a church for their faith, Christian service and joy in Christ. But he also challenged their complacent idleness in attitude and vulnerability to temptations of immoral conduct. He wanted to see them grow in Christ in the present as they work and wait patiently for His second coming for their promised eternal life with Him.

QUESTIONS FOR PERSONAL THOUGHT AND DISCUSSION

1. Read 1 Thess. 1:2-10—The Word Sounded Forth

a. In what two ways did the gospel come to the Thessalonians? (See 1 Thess. 1:4-5.)

b. In what way did the Thessalonians receive the gospel? (See 1 Thess. 1:6.)

c. To what places did the word "sound forth"? (See 1 Thess. 1:8.)

2. Read 1 Thess. 3:8-10—Live Now and Stand Fast

In what ways can we best live in the present? (See also 1 Thess. 2:9-12 and 4:11-12.)

_____

_____

3. Read 1 Thess. 4:1-12—God's Sanctification

Using Paul's words of instruction, describe God's will of sanctification. (See also 2 Cor. 3:18.)

_____

_____

_____

4. Read 1 Thess. 4:9-12—Believers and Outsiders

How are we to live among believers and "outsiders"?

_____

_____

_____

5. Read 1 Thess. 4:13-5:3—The Day of the Lord

a. How will Christ receive the dead and those still alive? (See also Matt. 24:29-31.)

_____

_____

b. When exactly does the Lord come? (See also Matt. 24:36.)

_____

_____

6. Read 1 Thess. 5:4-11—Waiting for Christ

In what ways are we to live while we wait for Christ's Second Coming?

_____

_____

7. Read 1 Thess. 5:12-26—Paul's Prayer

Carefully think of yourself as a Thessalonian, knowing Paul prayed this will of God for you. Which of these might you pray for yourself?

_____

_____

8. Read 2 Thess. 1:5-12—The Righteous Judgment

a. Describe the righteous judgment of God for the disobedient who do not know God. (See also 2 Thess. 2:9-12.)

b. Describe the righteous judgment of God for believers in the kingdom of God. (See also 2 Thess. 2:13-17.)

9. Read 2 Thess. 3:6-13—Idleness and Busybodies

a. How was idleness a problem, and how did it affect the sanctification of the believers?

b. How might we best spend our time serving Christ?

LESSON 25 SUMMARY

WAITING FOR CHRIST

1, 2 THESSALONIANS

Paul Called Christians to Wait Patiently for the Lord

The Thessalonians received these two letters commending them as a church for their faith, for their Christian ministry that *"has gone forth everywhere,"* and joy in Christ (1 Thess. 1). But he also challenged their complacent idleness in attitude and vulnerability to temptations of immoral conduct (1 Thess. 4). He wanted to see them grow in Christ as they work, serve in ministry and wait patiently for His second coming and their promised eternal life with Him (1 Thess. 5).

Paul clarified that judgment of the unrighteous is that of God at Christ's second coming (2 Thess. 1). Deceit by lawless ones is of Satan, and they will be condemned at Christ's judgment (2 Thess. 2). Therefore, the Thessalonian Christians were to stand firm in the gospel they had been taught. Paul warned them that idleness becomes a temptation to gossip, and become irresponsibe in their community. They were to work and wait patiently for their Lord (2 Thess. 3).

CONSIDER how God used Paul to strengthen the faith of the individual Thessalonians, and the church there as a whole. God wants for us the ability to live fruitfully in truth while we anticipate Christ's return to meet and be with Him eternally. Consider how the Spirit might sanctify you in a holy life to stand righteous before you Lord. Pray often for the strengths Paul prayed for the Thessalonians that you too might have strength through grace.

The Thessalonian Jews' hatred and persecutions of Christians caused Paul to leave for Berea (Acts 17), and then again to leave for Athens. It is probable that Paul again visited Thessalonica on his return to Jerusalem on his third mission trip in 56 A.D. (Acts 20).

Paul's First Letter Commended Their Faith

Paul wrote his first letter to the Thessalonians most likely while in Corinth about 49-51 A.D. while on his second mission trip. He had been in Thessalonica, Berea, and Athens (Acts 17) before arriving alone in Corinth. Timothy had been with him earlier in Athens, and probably went on to Thessalonica. Later, in Corinth, Timothy and Silas joined Paul (Acts 18). Timothy reported to Paul about the Thessalonian church and ministry (1 Thess. 3).

Thessalonica was the capital of the Roman province of Macedonia. It was a free city ruled by its own authorities (Acts 17). Paul had come to Thessalonica after Philippi on his second trip, and spent as much as three weeks there in the synagogue.

He also spent considerable time with Gentiles (1 Thess. 1-2; 2 Thess. 3; Philm. :4). His synagogue preaching was probably followed by other locations in the city.

The first letter dealt with special problems of these Christians, particularly their understanding of the second coming of Christ. Paul's love for these Christians was evident from his reference to their steadfast faith (1 Thess. 1-3). His joy over their faith and love was well known to other churches.

However, even as they were in Christ's likeness, they lived in an immoral society, and Paul showed concern for their spiritual welfare through his self-sacrificing ministry. Paul said, *"in all our distress and affliction we have been comforted about you through your faith. For now we live, if you are standing fast in the Lord,"* (1 Thess. 3:7-8).

Paul re-taught them the doctrine of sanctification, saying, *"may the Lord make you increase and abound in love for one another and for all, as we do for you, so that he may establish your hearts blameless in holiness before our God and Father, at the coming of our Lord Jesus with all his saints,"* (1 Thess. 3:12-13) and *"For the Lord himself will descend from heaven with a cry of command, with the voice of an archangel, and with the sound of the trumpet of God. And the dead in Christ will rise first. Then we who are alive, who are left, will be caught up together with them in the clouds to meet the Lord in the air, and so we will always be with the Lord. Therefore encourage one another with these words,"* (1 Thess. 4:16-18).

Their misunderstanding about the Christ's second coming led them to a weakened faith and erroneous doctrine (1 Thess. 4). He warned them to a life of discipline worthy of Christians living in the world, and in fellowship with each other (1 Thess. 4-5).

Paul's Second Letter Sought Patient Ministry

Paul's second letter was probably written shortly after the first. Its purpose was to correct the widespread misunderstanding of Paul's teaching about Christ's return.

Paul's salutation demonstrates that the Thessalonians were growing in their faith, love and steadfastness. He wrote, *"We ought always to give thanks to God for you, brothers, as is right, because your faith is growing abundantly, and the love of every one of you for one another is increasing. Therefore we ourselves boast about you in the churches of God for your steadfastness and faith in all your persecutions and in the afflictions that you are enduring,"* (2 Thess. 1:3-4).

The Thessalonians were disregarding what Paul had personally and explicitly taught them about Christ's second coming (2 Thess. 2-3), and what he had written in his previous letter.

The second letter contained severe warnings and commands, like his letter to the Galatians. Paul focused on the signs that will precede Christ's return. He stressed the ultimate manifestation of Satan's rebellion—*"the lawless one"*—in the apostasy and blasphemy that will occur beforehand (2 Thess. 2:3-12).

They thought that the great drama of Christ's return had already begun. Consequently, many of them had ceased working, thinking the end of the world was very near (2 Thess. 3). They were living in idleness, which was creating an embarrassing situation for Christians. Paul wrote, *"If anyone is not willing to work, let him not eat. For we hear that some among you walk in idleness, not busy at work, but busybodies. Now such persons we command and encourage in the Lord Jesus Christ to do their work quietly and to earn their own living,"* (2 Thess. 3:10-12).

Paul's second letter reprimanded this inaction and commanded them to continue steadfastly in true teaching, imitating his own example of work while he was with them. His exhortation was to pray, continue in the faith, and discipline those in error as brothers and sisters in Christ. Paul sharply reprimanded the idlers and instructed the church to withdraw from them in love. *"Do not regard him as an enemy, but warn him as a brother,"* he said (2 Thess. 3:15).

This advice would help prepare all of them for strong faith until Christ's return. The Christian response is to stand firm in truth of the gospel, working and ministering quietly in good standing with all.

CONSIDER how God brought light into the world at creation, and brought your Light into your world as your Savior and Redeemer. Paul wrote, *"But you are not in darkness, brothers, for that day to surprise you like a thief. For you are all children of light, children of the day. We are not of the night or of the darkness. But since we belong to the day, let us be sober, having put on the breastplate of faith and love, and for a helmet the hope of salvation. For God has not destined us for wrath, but to obtain salvation through our Lord Jesus Christ, who died for us so that whether we are awake or asleep we might live with him. Therefore encourage one another and build one another up, just as you are doing,"* (1 Thess. 5:4-5, 8-11).

GIFTS AND LEADERSHIP

1, 2 TIMOTHY, TITUS AND PHILEMON

These four books demonstrate God's concern for His leaders and their gifts, and thus, for His Church and the world. Paul equipped Timothy, Titus and Philemon with leadership principles and specific instruction for the strengthening of fellowship. These books demonstrate the need and value of leadership and wise use of gifts, as well as the need for pastoral care for church leaders.

QUESTIONS FOR PERSONAL THOUGHT AND DISCUSSION

1. Read 1 Tim. 1:3-7—Myths and Genealogies

a. According to Paul, how could Christian teachers' interests in "myths and human genealogies" promote false doctrines? (See also 2 Tim. 4:3-4.)

b. From your experience, what are some religious teachings today that are contrary to Christ's gospel of salvation in Him?

2. Read 1 Tim. 2:1-6—Pray for Leaders of Nations

Of the whole world, for whom are we to pray especially?
Who does God desire to be saved?

3. Scan 1 Tim. 3—Leaders' Faith and Godliness

How are leaders to be "pillars and buttresses of truth" for the
church? What does it mean to be "manifested in the flesh"
and "vindicated by the Spirit"?

4. Read 1 Tim. 4:4-14—Don't Neglect Your Gifts

What are some acceptable "godly gifts" that you might use?

5. Read 1 Tim. 6:6-10—Godliness and Contentment

What is Paul's advice about desiring riches and tempting
cravings.

6. Read 2 Tim. 1:6-14—God's Spirit is Powerful

Describe the "spirit" God gave you. How might you demonstrate that power and love?

7. Read 2 Tim. 2:1-10—Suffer for the Gospel

How are we to "suffer as a soldier, athlete or farmer" for Christ?

8. Read 2 Tim. 2:22-26—Flee Youthful Passions

Who grants repentance and knowledge of the truth? How does one pursue righteousness?

9. Read 2 Tim. 3:12-17—All Scripture Is Inspired

How can we *"be wise for salvation"*?

10. Read Titus 1:10-16—Some Teachers Deny God

How might one profess to know God but deny Him by his works? (See also Luke 9: 23 and 1 John 2:4-6.)

11. Titus 2:1-8—Older Believers Lead Younger

How might younger Christians learn from older ones? Why?

12. Titus 3:4-11—Renounce Ungodliness

How does the grace of God train us to renounce ungodliness?

13. Read Philm. :8-16—Equality in Christ

Using the word slave for "bondservant," why was it important that Philemon forgive in Christ his runaway slave Onesimus?

LESSON 26 SUMMARY

GIFTS AND LEADERSHIP

1, 2 TIMOTHY, TITUS AND PHILEMON

Paul's Letters on Leaders and Leadership

Paul often focused on his leaders—delegating and training for the growing ministries. He had confidence in Timothy's gifts, and gave guidance for his success as a church leader through his first letter about the church and the gifts of God's stewards and duties of church leaders (1 Tim.). He wrote to Timothy again (2 Tim.) while longing for a Christian companion. He counseled Timothy to *"keep aflame the gift that is within him,"* and not to fear persecution and suffering.

Paul instructed Titus, God's steward at Crete, to utilize the church's gifts for Crete's church organization, elders, deacons, and to prevent false teaching and immoral conduct (Titus). His letter to Philemon was to further the usefulness of a new Christian servant for God's use, bringing Christian equality between master and servant into the church and as a contrast to the world around them (Philm.).

CONSIDER how God gives us leaders and ways to lead with various gifts for stewardship in His church. Consider how the Holy Spirit was poured out at Pentecost to spread the Gospel, and equip leaders to minister to all ends of the earth. Pray about how God might use you and your gifts as you too are blessed to be a blessing!

Paul's First Letter to Timothy on Church Leaders

This first letter is about the church and the gifts of God's stewards, their qualifications, and duties of church officers. Timothy had considerable respect and authority, and was carefully instructed on organizing this local body of Christians. He was called "minister" and was instructed how to enforce the truth of Christ's gospel in teaching.

Paul wrote this letter to Timothy and another to Titus most likely after his first two-year imprisonment in Rome (Titus 3:12).

Timothy was in Ephesus (1 Tim. 1). Paul repeated his desire to visit Timothy (1 Tim. 3). Timothy's ministry assignment was very difficult. While Paul had confidence in him and his gifts, he felt he needed guidance and help if he were to succeed.

Timothy was to lead and supervise worship (1 Tim. 2, 4). Paul guided Timothy to regulate apparel and conduct of women, particularly not to disrupt worship (1 Tim. 2). Timothy was to instruct and supervise the organization of the church with ministers, called "bishops," "deacons" and "elders." He was to be an example in personal conduct of purity and holiness in all things (1 Tim. 4-6).

The minister was to deal with old and young, men and women (1 Tim. 5). Leaders were to care for widows (1 Tim. 5). Paul counseled Timothy to appoint qualified elders, and to rebuke elders who sin (1 Tim. 5). Paul then gave Timothy perspectives for the church and its leaders about possessions and money (1 Tim. 6).

Paul's Second Letter to Timothy on Strength

Paul's second letter to Timothy was written after the first, and another to Titus, from prison in Rome (2 Tim. 1). He wrote shortly before his martyred death during Nero's reign. He indicated no hope of release from prison (2 Tim. 4), and felt deserted by friends and sensed the end of his life (2 Tim. 1-4). Luke alone was with him (2 Tim. 4). Paul longed to see Timothy, and asked that he bring Mark with him also (2 Tim. 4). In a practical request, he asked for a warm winter coat as well as books and writing parchment. He recalled his past persecution and sufferings (2 Tim. 3) and spoke bitterly of his friends' failure to support him in his first trial (2 Tim. 4).

Paul's "pastor's heart" was saddened as he thought about the welfare of his beloved new converts and the dangers they encountered from false teaching (2 Tim. 2-4). He counseled Timothy to *"keep aflame the gift that is within him,"* (2 Tim. 1:6), and not to fear persecution and suffering.

Paul said that grace is sufficient, so *"be strong in the grace that is in Christ Jesus,"* (2 Tim. 2:1). As a good soldier or hard-working farmer, Paul said, the Christian is to be singularly-focused, not to get entangled in distractions. He is to stay with the sound doctrine he has been taught (2 Tim. 1-3) and to preach the message with conviction and power (2 Tim. 4).

Paul's Letter to Titus

The Titus letter was probably written between the two letters to Timothy, from Macedonia. Titus was supervising churches on the island of Crete (Titus 1:5), and Paul was on his way to Nicopolis, in Achaia on the Adriatic Sea (3:12). Paul was apparently arrested there and sent back to Rome. Crete's church organization (Titus 1:5), false teaching (1:10-11, 14-16), and immoral conduct were Paul's concerns.

This letter instructs Titus, God's steward over Christians at Crete, to utilize the church's gifts. Titus, like Timothy, is charged with considerable responsibility at Crete, with the authority to appoint elders in the various churches on the island (Titus 1:5).

He is told to rebuke false teachers (Titus 1:13; 3:10) and raise up faithful mentors. Paul said, *"teach what accords with sound doctrine. Older men are to be sober-minded, dignified, self-controlled, sound in faith, in love, and in steadfastness. Older women likewise are to be reverent in behavior, not slanderers or slaves to much wine. They are to teach what is good, and so train the young women,"* (Titus 2:1-4a).

Titus is told to exhort and reprove with all authority (Titus 2:15; 3:8) and exercise spiritual and teaching oversight over the churches. *"Let no one disregard you,"* (Titus 2:15) is Paul's advice. Everyone in the church needs instruction in Christian living (Titus 2). Christians are to respect authorities (Titus 3) and live at peace with all men. Controversies and senseless debates are to be avoided. Dissenters who persist in their factiousness are to be banished.

Paul's Letter to Philemon

Paul's letter to Philemon was written from a prison in Rome about 59-61 A.D. The church met in Philemon's home where the letter was shared by all of them. It seems that Philemon was close to Paul and converted through his ministry (Philm. :19).

The letter was primarily about Christian forgiveness of slave by master. Onesimus, a slave, had fled from his master Philemon to Rome, where he was also converted through Paul's ministry. Paul wanted him to return to his master, and sent this letter along, perhaps by Tychicus, who was to accompany Onesimus (Col. 4:7-9). Paul implored this Christian leader to demonstrate Christ's forgiveness by no longer judging former deeds or relationships.

In returning Onesimus to his master, Paul promised to pay whatever Onesimus owed Philemon (Philm. :18-19). Paul wrote for his friend to receive Onesimus back not merely as a slave, but as a brother in Christ (Philm. :16-17). Now that he was a believer, he was really *"more useful"* than before to the fellowship of believers (Philm. :11). This was a pun on the name Onesimus which means "useful." Paul's plea is for Philemon to further the usefulness of a servant for God's use.

CONSIDER how Paul wrote, *"All Scripture is breathed out by God and profitable for teaching, for reproof, for correction, and for training in righteousness, that the man of God may be complete, equipped for every good work,"* (2 Tim. 3:16). Praises to our Savior for His Holy Word!

FAITH

HEBREWS

The letter to "the Hebrews" is to all Hebrews everywhere, as no persons or groups are named. *"To the Hebrews"* was added later to the text based upon the content. The writer of Hebrews—possibly Paul or another early-church minister—was trying to convince the Jewish ethnics to see how a faith life in Christ lets them know and trust God. It is through knowing God that we know who we are supposed to be. The writer spent a lot of time describing Christ and comparing Him to all of the other avenues the Jews used to relate to God.

QUESTIONS FOR PERSONAL THOUGHT AND DISCUSSION

1. Read Heb. 1:1-4—*"God has Spoken to Us"*

a. Describe how God *"has spoken to us"* through the prophets. (See also page 113-114.)

b. Describe how God has spoken to us through His Son.

2. Read Heb. 2:1-4—Stay Focused on the Message

How might one drift away from the message of salvation?

_____

_____

3. Read Heb. 4:9-16—Sabbath Rest

a. When is the Sabbath "rest" for the people of God?

_____

_____

b. How might one enter that rest?

_____

_____

c. Describe the word of God and its role.

_____

_____

d. In what ways is Jesus our High Priest?

_____

_____

4. Read Heb. 5:11-6:3—Mature in the Word

a. What does it mean to be "dull of hearing" and "unskilled in the word of righteousness"?

_____

_____

b. How can we progress in doctrine to maturity?

_____

_____

5. Read Heb. 6:9-20—Assurance of Salvation

According to Hebrews, how can one be assured of salvation in Christ Jesus?

_____

6. Read Heb. 8:1-7 and 9:15-22—Jesus' Covenant

a. Compare the Old Covenant to Jesus' New Covenant.

_____

_____

b. Read Jeremiah 31:33-34. Describe Jeremiah's prophesy.

_____

7. Read Heb. 10:5-14—Sacrificed Once for All

Describe God's plan to end earthly sacrifices and establish a single offering.

8. Read Heb. 11:1-3 and Gal. 2:16—Faith

a. Using these verses, define "faith" in your own words.

b. Compare "belief," "faith" and "justification."

9. Read Heb. 12:1-2—The Founder and Perfecter

a. How is Christ the "founder" of our faith?

b. How is He the "perfecter" of our faith?

LESSON 27 SUMMARY

FAITH

HEBREWS

Faith in Christ Is Better

The writer of Hebrews was trying to convince the Jewish ethnics to see how a faith life in Christ lets them know and trust God. It is through knowing God that we know who we are supposed to be. The writer spent a great deal of time describing Christ and comparing Him to all of the other avenues the Jews used to relate to God.

The author of this letter-sermon to the Hebrews is often presumed to be Paul, although not identified anywhere in the scripture. While the content and references are consistent with those of Paul, the style and order are quite different.

The letter is written much like a sermon that was then re-written as a letter. Frequent homiletic devices of the book support the sermon origin (Heb. 5, 6, 9). Possible writers or transcribers, if Paul delivered the sermon, are Luke, Apollos, or Barnabas.

CONSIDER how through knowing God, we know who we are supposed to be. A faith life through Christ lets us know and trust God. Through knowing God we learn who our Creator designed us to be. Through trusting Him we assent to His will and bear His image. Consider how God calls us to know, believe, and confess our Lord in Christ.

Praise Him that in His redemption we are forgiven, justified, and counted as righteous before God. In faith we ask God to be transformed to Jesus Christ's image.

The Hebrews are general recipients of the letter, including *"they of Italy."* It doesn't differentiate those living "in" or "out" of Italy. Hebrews were dispersed geographically between 70 and 90 A.D.

These readers were Jewish Christians in danger of abandoning their faith and slipping back into Judaism because of the growing criticism and opposition to them as Christians. He exhorted them to hold fast to their confession in Christ as Savior and Lord (Heb. 4 and 10). They needed to mature in their faith and be more committed in their actions.

The author called his writing a brief word of exhortation (Heb. 13) because of the danger of being persecuted. Christian persecution had not yet reached death by martyrdom (Heb. 12), but was severe nevertheless (Heb. 10). He warned not to neglect Christ's message of salvation which they had heard and believed (Heb. 2).

Christ Is Better

The writer, trying to convince the Jews of how a faith life in Christ could let them know and trust God, described Christ and compared Him to all of the other avenues the Jews used to relate to God.

The writer said Christ is better than angels, prophets, patriarchs, and priests. In earlier times, God spoke through prophets and now through Christ. He wrote, *"Long ago, at many times and in many ways, God spoke to our fathers by the prophets, but in these last days he has spoken to us by his Son, whom he appointed the heir of all things, through whom also he created the world.*

"He is the radiance of the glory of God and the exact imprint of his nature, and he upholds the universe by the word of his power. After making purification for sins, he sat down at the right hand of the Majesty on high, having become as much superior to angels as the name he has inherited is more excellent than theirs," (Heb. 1:1-4).

Christ Is Better than Patriarchs and Prophets

Making an apologetic case for Christ, the writer asked why the Israelites were so rebellious, even though they had learned under Moses. They were unable to enter Canaan because of unbelief. (Heb. 3). He continued, *"For good news came to us just as to them, but the message they heard did not benefit them, because they were not united by faith with those who listened. For we who have believed enter that rest,"* (Heb. 4:1-3a).

He encouraged the Hebrews to *"enter the rest"* in Christ, *"For the word of God is living and active, sharper than any two-edged sword, piercing to the division of soul and of spirit, of joints and of marrow, and discerning the thoughts and intentions of the heart. And no creature is hidden from his sight, but all are naked and exposed to the eyes of him to whom we must give account,"* (Heb. 4:12-13).

Christ Is Better than the Earthly High Priests

He said, *"Since then we have a great high priest who has passed through the heavens, Jesus, the Son of God, let us hold fast our confession. For we do not have a high priest who is unable to sympathize with our weaknesses, but one who in every respect has been tempted as we are, yet without sin. Let us then with confidence draw near to the throne of grace, that we may receive mercy and find grace to help in time of need,"* (Heb. 4:14-16).

He accused the Hebrew Christians of becoming *"dull of hearing. For ...you need someone to teach you again the basic principles of the oracles of God. You need milk, not solid food, for everyone who lives on milk is unskilled in the word of righteousness, since he is a child. But solid food is for the mature, for those who have their powers of discernment trained by constant practice to distinguish good from evil,"* (Heb. 5:11b-14).

"For it was indeed fitting that we should have such a high priest, holy, innocent, unstained, separated from sinners, and exalted above the heavens. He has no need, like those high priests, to offer sacrifices daily, first for his own sins and then for those of the people, since he

did this once for all when he offered up himself. For the law appoints men in their weakness as high priests, but the word of the oath, which came later than the law, appoints a Son who has been made perfect forever," (Heb. 7:26-28).

Christ's Covenant Is Better

He described Jesus as our High Priest of a "better covenant." The old sacrifices were repetitious, therefore each individually was ineffective—only symbols of the perfect Christ to come. He said, *"we have such a high priest, one who is seated at the right hand of the throne of the Majesty in heaven, a minister in the holy places, in the true tent that the Lord set up, not man. For every high priest is appointed to offer gifts and sacrifices; thus it is necessary for this priest also to have something to offer. ... But as it is, Christ has obtained a ministry that is as much more excellent than the old as the covenant he mediates is better, since it is enacted on better promises. For if that first covenant had been faultless, there would have been no occasion to look for a second. ... In speaking of a new covenant, he makes the first one obsolete. And what is becoming obsolete and growing old is ready to vanish away,"* (Heb. 8:1b-3, 6-7, 13).

Christ is better. His purpose is not judgment but mercy. His mercy was offered once for all time, and for all sins of those with faith. Faith is the better way—to know God through Christ. Like that *"great cloud of witnesses,"* before us (Heb. 12), faith in Christ gives us knowledge, assurance and conviction to know God is our Savior (Heb. 10). Christ is forever (Heb. 13). Through our faith, our understanding is clear, blessings are given, God's earthly plan unfolds, fear and pain are go away, miracles happen in our lives, and victories are won (Heb. 11).

CONSIDER how, in this Christian faith, we seek the knowledge of God, assent to His will, and place our trust in His plan for our lives. As knowledge, assent, and trust are necessary parts of faith, pray today for God's truth to be known, believed, and lived in your world.

SANCTIFICATION AND GOOD WORKS

JAMES AND 1, 2 PETER

These books on sanctification show that: trials lead to strengthened faith (James); Christians are sanctified through pure living (1 Pet.); and with knowledge we know God and must live in the truth (2 Pet.). In these letters we see how God leads us through the process of sanctification in our life.

Through ever-changing sanctification, we draw ever closer to God. While justification is God's one-time gift of salvation by grace through faith alone, sanctification follows, and is the process of dying more and more to sin and growing in Christ after being made new (2 Pet. 3).

QUESTIONS FOR PERSONAL THOUGHT AND DISCUSSION

1. Read James 1:1-4, 12—Strength From Trials

What might a Christian expect from "meeting trials of various kinds"?

2. Read James 1:12-18—God Tempts No One

Can God be tempted and can He tempt us? From where does temptation come?

3. Read James 1:19-25—Doers, Not Hearers Only

a. What five things might we do to prepare to "be doers of the word"? (See James 1:19-21.)

b. Describe a "hearer-only." (See James 1:22-24.)

c. Describe a "doer who acts." (See James 1:25.)

4. Read James 2:14-26—Faith Without Works

a. Describe faith with no works. (See James 2:14-17.)

b. Describe faith with works. (See James 2:18-26.)

5. Read James 3:13-18—Wisdom from Above

Compare earthly wisdom to the fruits of godly wisdom.

6. Read 1 Pet. 1:3-9 and John 3:3-8—Born Again

Describe the meaning and purpose of being "born again."

7. Read 1 Pet. 2:18-25—Doing Good and Enduring

Read verse 21. How might we follow in Christ's steps, submitting to employers or others in authority?

8. Read 1 Pet. 5:1-6—God Exalts the Humble

a. Describe God's view of the proud, versus the humble.

b. What happens when we "cast all our anxieties on Him"?

9. Read 1 Pet. 5:6-11—Satan Prowls Like a Lion

a. What are some things we can do to resist Satan?

b. What four things will God do?

10. Read 2 Pet. 1:2-11—Supplement Your Faith

a. From what have we escaped and why? (See 2 Pet. 1:4.)

b. What are seven supplements for our faith?

11. Read 2 Pet. 3:8-10—The Lord is Patient with You

Describe God's sense of timing, and His patience.

12. Read 2 Pet. 3:14-18—Be Diligent and Grow

Considering these three letters of James and Peter, what are some ways that you might grow in God's grace and knowledge?

SANCTIFICATION AND GOOD WORKS

JAMES AND 1, 2 PETER

James' and Peter's Letters on Sanctification

In these letters we see how God leads us through the process of sanctification in our life. Through ever-changing sanctification, we draw even closer to God.

Justification is God's one-time gift of salvation by grace through faith alone (Rom. 3, Eph. 2, Gal. 3). Sanctification follows, and is the process of change after being made new (2 Cor. 3-4; 2 Pet. 3). We are born again (1 Pet. 1) to live no longer by human passions but by God's will (1 Pet. 4).

Paul also described Christian sanctification, saying, *"And we all, with unveiled face, beholding the glory of the Lord, are being transformed into the same image from one degree of glory to another. For this comes from the Lord who is the Spirit,"* (2 Cor. 3:18). Another translation says we are transformed *"degree by degree into his likeness,"* (RSV). Sanctification allows us to become, over our lives, more and more like Christ, bearing His image.

CONSIDER how God can't tempt anyone with evil, certainly not us! But He allows us to be strengthened as we resist and overcome temptation and sin in our lives! Consider how He redeemed us in total forgiveness, but then sanctifies us to stand righteous before God as His image bearers! The Creator Father sends wisdom from above, and builds our faith to be capable of good works. Sanctified, we are indeed *"blessed to be a blessing."*

James Taught Sanctification by Faith with Works

The author James is presumed to be the brother of Christ. Christ's brothers did not believe in Him during His ministry, but after the ascension they were active with the Jerusalem church. James was a pillar of the church in Jerusalem that hosted the Jerusalem conference on legalism and Gentile Christianity (Acts 15). Paul spoke of the risen Christ's appearance to James (1 Cor. 15), who had become a leader in this church and died a martyr for Christ in 62 A.D. James referred to himself as teacher (James 3), and wrote the letter in about 45 A.D.

Trials from Temptation Strengthen Faith

James wrote that withstanding trials from temptation leads to strengthened faith, which shows in works. We receive wisdom—but not temptation—from God in prayer for ourselves and one another. God cannot be tempted, and in His graciousness tempts no one.

James describes an "upward spiral," saying the steadfast man who endures trials will receive the *"crown of life."* And he presents a "downward spiral," saying one's own sinful desire leads to temptation, then gives birth to sin, and "fully grown" sin brings death (James 1).

In order to have *"the righteousness of God"* James warns to avoid the initial evil deceit of Satan. He says to *"put away all filthiness"* and look to the Father above. We are to be *"doers of the word,"* (James 1).

Faith without Works is a Dead Faith

James said we are to avoid and cease partiality, or selfish discrimination, and do good works that prove faith because *"faith by itself, if it does not have works, is dead...For as the body apart from the spirit is dead, so also faith apart from works is dead,"* (James 2).

Being sanctified with the *"wisdom from above,"* we are to control our tongues and demonstrate godly wisdom in good conduct and works (James 3). We must distance the world, humble ourselves and be dependent on God (James 4). He wrote, *"Resist the devil, and he will flee from you. Draw near to God, and he will draw near to you,"* (James 4:7-8). We are to fear wealth and wait for Christ with an enduring faith, pray for others who are afflicted, and help Christian brethren who err in sin (James 5).

Peter Shared His Witness of Christ's Suffering

Peter the apostle introduced himself as *"a fellow elder and witness of the sufferings of Jesus Christ,"* (1 Pet. 5). He wrote from "Babylon," probably meaning Rome. His scribe was Silvanus (1 Pet. 5), probably the same as Silas in Acts. Mark was with him (likely John Mark of Acts 12:25). Since Peter died in 64 or 67 A.D., this letter was probably written in the early sixties. Peter wrote to the Christians who lived in the Roman provinces of Pontus, Galatia, Cappadocia, Asia, and Bithynia, all in northern Asia (1 Pet. 1).

Peter Calls for Sanctification through Purity

Peter explained that they had been born again in Christ, and encouraged these Christians that they are sanctified through pure living. They are being guarded through faith for salvation, and receive blessings of hope, joy, freedom, and confidence. God cares for, restores, and strengthens them (1 Pet. 1).

Peter exhorted them to *"grow up to salvation"* in purity and spirituality, and to abstain from malice, envy, slander (1 Pet. 2), and other carnal passions of heathen living. He said, *"you are a chosen race, a royal priesthood, a holy nation, a people for his own possession,"* (1 Pet. 2:9). God's people are to use Christian liberty to live as God's servants, with sympathy, love, humility (1 Pet. 5), hospitality (1 Pet. 4), and unity of the brethren (1 Pet. 3). The letter reflects suffering and trial. Readers had already undergone persecution, but further trials awaited them. Their authorities are not blamed, but rather the Christians are exhorted to be subject to them and honor their masters or employers with mindful respect (1 Pet. 2).

In suffering, Christians are to follow Christ's example using their gifts for the mutual welfare. In everything they are sanctified by God who is glorified through Christ (1 Pet. 2). Any trials are occasion for joy and witness. God cares for His own and will strengthen them (1 Pet. 4).

Peter's Second Letter on Growing in Grace of God

Peter wrote that, *"His divine power has given us everything we need for a godly life through our knowledge of him who called us by his own glory and goodness,"* (2 Pet. 1). God wishes that all will repent, and all will know the truth (2 Pet. 3). We must live in this truth.

The letter is a reminder of the truth of the gospel for the Christians' growing strength against the world and against false teachers (2 Pet. 1). God will punish those who *"exploit you with fabricated stories,"* (2 Pet. 2). False teachers were corrupt and immoral (2 Pet. 2, 3, 10), carousing and defiled by the world and its passions.

True knowledge reveals God and His offer of salvation, by which believers receive power of the Holy Spirit. Those are enabled to forsake sin and confirm the call through sanctification (2 Pet. 1:16-19).

The Christian faith is based on personal witness of the majesty of Christ. Peter said that God will keep His promise of return, so we are warned to keep spotless and pure. We are to grow in the grace and knowledge of the Lord (2 Pet. 3). Paul taught that sanctification is the process of change in being made new (2 Cor. 3:18). We are born again (1 Pet. 1) to live no longer by human passions but by God's will (1 Pet. 4).

CONSIDER how God sanctifies us after our new birth into Christ. This produces a hunger and thirst to know more of God's will, and the strength of the Holy Spirit to be transformed into the likeness of Christ. Praises to God for His mercy and grace that we can become His image-bearers in Christ!

DISCERNING TRUTH

1, 2, 3 JOHN AND JUDE

These short letters demonstrate that God draws this world to His truth by denouncing false teaching, promoting truth, and strengthening His teachers with Christ's gospel. Dangerous philosophies that are taught rob the Christian faith of Christ's distinct gospel message (1 John).

John attacked the heretical teaching that Christ was not a man in the flesh (1 John and 2 John). John's third letter was written to provide help and care for Christian teachers of truth ministering between churches (3 John). Jude also wrote about issues of heresy and false teaching, and about remaining true to the faith (Jude).

QUESTIONS FOR PERSONAL THOUGHT AND DISCUSSION

1. Read 1 John 1:1-4 and John 20:24-29—John the Apostle and Christ's Eyewitness

a. What value did John bring as an eyewitness to Christ?

b. How did Thomas overcome his doubt? What was Christ's wish for those who would never see His human form?

2. Read 1 John 1:5-7—Walking in the Light

a. What are characteristics of those who walk in darkness?

b. Describe those who walk in the light. (See also John 1:6-14.)

3. Read 1 John 1:8-1 John 2:6—All Are Sinners

Who are sinners and what is the solution? (See also Rom. 3:10-12, 20.)

4. Read 1 John 2:21-26—Antichrists Deny Christ

What specifically did these false teachers deny?

5. Read 1 John 4:1-6—Test the Spirits

How are we to know false teaching from Christ's truth?

6. Read 1 John 5:6-12—The Role of the Holy Spirit

a. What is the role of the Holy Spirit? (See also John 16:13-15.)

_____

_____

b. What is the "Spirit of truth"?

_____

_____

c. What is the "testimony of truth"? (See 1 John 5:11-12.)

_____

_____

7. Read 2 John :4-6—Walking in Truth

a. How are we to walk in truth?

_____

_____

b. What are Jesus' two great commandments? (See Matt. 22:34-40.)

_____

_____

8. Read 3 John :9-11—Welcoming Missionaries

Who do you think these teachers are, and how would supporting them be helpful?

_____

_____

9. Read Jude :1-9—Immorality and Denying Christ

a. What false teaching today might give a "license for immorality"?

_____

_____

b. What are some examples Jude gives in verses 5-13?

_____

_____

c. Describe Enoch's prophesy. (See verses 14-16.)

_____

10. Read Jude :20-21—Persevere in Evil Times

What are some ways Jude says we can persevere?

_____

_____

LESSON 1 SUMMARY

DISCERNING TRUTH

1, 2, 3 JOHN AND JUDE

John and Jude Urged to Reject Heresy, Hold Truth

These short letters demonstrate that God draws this world to His truth by testing and denouncing false teaching, and by supporting and promoting His truth and His teachers of Christ's gospel. Philosophies that don't reflect Christ's gospel are dangerous and rob the Christian faith of His distinctive message (1 John).

John attacked the heretical teaching that Christ was fully human and also fully God (1 John 4 and 2 John 1). John's third letter was written to solve problems of Christian teachers who taught true doctrine ministering between several churches. They should be warmly welcomed, cared for, and helped in their travels (3 John).

Jude also wrote to the issues of heresy, false teaching, and remaining true to the faith (Jude).

CONSIDER how God draws this world to His truth through a testing and denouncement of false teaching, and in support and promotion of His gospel truth. Consider how God the Father sent His Son to relate to us in every way, giving us His gospel of salvation. And upon His ascension He sent His Spirit of Truth to assure our testimony of His gospel. Pray for God's discernment of

His teaching, and ways you might help others discern the truth of Jesus Christ. Praises to the Creator of Light who came that we might walk in His Light and be His blessing!

Philosophies that don't reflect Christ's truth and His Christian message are dangerous (1 John). Central to these books is the warning against any teaching that denies Christ's gospel of justification by the Savior who is fully man and fully God. John attacked the heretical teaching that Christ was not God who came as a man in the flesh (1 John 4:2-3 and 2 John 1:7).

Gnostics of that period conceived and taught that there is a fundamental "split" between the spiritual and material worlds. The Gnostic would say that since the material world is evil, and since the human body is part of the material world, God in Christ would not appear in a body of evil. Their conclusion was that Christ came as a ghost—denying that Jesus came in the flesh.

John Assured the Truth of Christ and His Gospel

The author is the apostle John, though the letter does not bear his name. He wrote as an eyewitness of the person and ministry of Christ. His words are strongly reminiscent of the Gospel of John. The tone implies that he was an old man.

The first letter is dated around 90 A.D., perhaps from Ephesus. It is to a general audience addressing *"children"* and *"little children,"* *"brethren"* and *"beloved."* He recalled the fundamentals of the Christian faith, and assured the reality of salvation based on Christ's sacrifice, *"that you may know that you have eternal life,"* (1 John 5).

John boldly asserted that that Christian conviction rests on Christ becoming flesh, and that many on earth were eyewitnesses to His coming. All else that is taught is delusive doctrine (2 John). John as an eyewitness and friend of Christ wrote, *"That which was from the beginning, which we have heard, which we have seen with our eyes, which we looked upon and have touched with our hands, concerning the word of life—the life was made manifest, and we have seen it, and testify to it and proclaim to you the eternal life,"* (1 John 1:1-2).

John wrote his letters so that Christians wouldn't sin, and warned of those people that would lead them into sinful activity. He described the false teacher as, *"he who denies that Jesus is the Christ...No one who denies the Son has the Father. He who confesses the Son has the Father also,"* (1 John 2).

He implored righteous living, saying, *"Little children, let no one deceive you. Whoever practices righteousness is righteous, as he is righteous. Whoever makes a practice of sinning is of the devil, for the devil has been sinning from the beginning. The reason the Son of God appeared was to destroy the works of the devil. No one born of God makes a practice of sinning, for God's seed abides in him; and he cannot keep on sinning, because he has been born of God,"* (1 John 3:7-9).

John's Second and Third Letters Call for Truth

John emphasized the importance of love in Christian fellowship (2 John :5-6). He warned of the heresy of those who deny the incarnation of Jesus Christ (2 John :7). These deceivers were the antichrist, claiming their teaching as superior and above the Christian message (2 John :9). Such false teachers should not even be received at home (2 John :10-11).

John's third letter was written to resolve problems of Christian teachers who taught the true doctrine ministering between churches. This is a personal letter addressed to Gaius (not necessarily the ones mentioned in Acts, Rom. or 1 Cor.), a leader in a local church.

The Christian teachers should be warmly welcomed, cared for, and supported (3 John). He said, *"Therefore we ought to support people like these, that we may be fellow workers for the truth,"* (3 John :8).

Diotrephes, presumably the local leader, refused to receive these Christian teachers, rejected the elder's authority and expelled those in the church who welcomed them. So John wrote to his good friend Gaius, urging him to help the teachers. Demetrius (3 John :12) may have delivered the letter, or may have been a church member there.

Jude Calls to Reject the Ungodly and Build Faith

The writer identified himself as *"Jude, a servant of Jesus Christ and a brother of James"* (Jude :1), which could mean the birth-brother of Christ (Mark 6). Most of Jude is reproduced in 2 Peter. The readers were not identified and the letter is to Christians in general.

Jude also wrote to the issues of heretical false teaching (Jude :3-4). False teachers, having the Gnostic philosophy, were perverting the grace of God into licentiousness and denying the lordship of Christ (Jude :4). They were teaching sexual impurity, rejection of authority, and reviling in spiritual powers (Jude :8).

These worldly people were causing division in the church (Jude :19) with their flagrant immorality and passions (Jude :10-16). By denying that sins of the flesh could affect the welfare of the soul, they modeled and taught immoral behavior. It had become urgent that they be exposed and their evil teachings condemned.

Jude wrote, *"But, dear friends, remember what the apostles of our Lord Jesus Christ foretold. They said to you, 'In the last times there will be scoffers who will follow their own ungodly desires.' These are the people who divide you, who follow mere natural instincts and do not have the Spirit,"* (Jude :17-19).

He encouraged them to build *"yourselves up in your most holy faith and praying in the Holy Spirit, keep yourselves in God's love as you wait for the mercy of our Lord Jesus Christ to bring you to eternal life,"* (Jude :20-21).

CONSIDER Jude's prayer for you in discerning truth: *"To him who is able to keep you from stumbling and to present you before his glorious presence without fault and with great joy—to the only God our Savior be glory, majesty, power and authority, through Jesus Christ our Lord, before all ages, now and forevermore! Amen,"* (Jude :24-25).

GLORIFICATION AND OVERCOMING EVIL

REVELATION

God ends the Bible story with Christ's return in full glory, in victorious defeat of Satan. It is the person of Christ that dominates the book of Revelation—the Lamb *"as though it had been slain"* (Rev. 5), and the Warrior who goes forth to conquer and rule, whose name is *"The Word of God,"* (Rev. 19). John gave to all of mankind God's vision of the risen and glorified Christ (Rev. 1).

Christ demonstrated both encouragement and challenges through letters to seven churches with evaluations of their faith (Rev. 2-3). We are shown visions of the ever-worsening persecution of the universal church by Satan and his evil ones (Rev. 4-11). Christ steps in and battles evil for His believers (Rev. 12-19). The most important fact for our world and life eternal lies in Christ's final victory over Satan and all evil (19-20). Heaven is shown rejoicing (Rev. 20-22).

QUESTIONS FOR PERSONAL THOUGHT AND DISCUSSION

1. Read Rev. 1:1-3—John's Commissioning

a. Whose revelation was given and to whom? Who first gave or authorized the revelation?

b. Who are the end recipients and what are they to learn?

c. Who was the messenger to John? What was his role?

d. What is promised to those who read, hear and keep it?

e. Read Rev. 1:9-11. Describe John's description of his partnership with the churches.

f. On what day and in what spiritual state did he receive the visions? What was the message?

2. Read Rev. 2:1-11—Letters to Ephesus and Smyrna

a. Describe the commendations and the actions requested of the Ephesians.

b. Describe the commendations and the actions requested of the Christians at Smyrna.

3. Read Rev. 3:14-22—Counsel to the Laodiceans

Describe the commendations and the actions requested of the Christians at Laodicea.

4. Read Rev. 4:1-11—First View of Heaven

a. Who do you think might be seated on the center throne?

_____

b. Who were the ones seated on the surrounding thrones, and how many?

_____

_____

c. From verses 8 and 11, and 5:9-14, who all were there and what were they saying?

_____

_____

5. Read Rev. 7:9-17 and Acts 1:8—All Nations

Describe the crowd of worshipers around the throne, and compare with Jesus' promise at His ascension.

_____

_____

6. Read Rev. 11:15-18—The Seventh Trumpet

Describe the change on earth that is announced.

_____

7. Read Rev. 14:1-5 and John 1:29—The Lamb and the Redeemed

a. Who might the Lamb be?

_____

b. Describe their song and their redemption.

_____

_____

8. Read Rev. 3: 5 and 20:7-15—Defeat of Satan and Judgment

a. What happens to those whose names are in the book of life?

_____

b. What happens to Satan?

_____

c. What happens to any whose name is not in the book of life?

_____

9. Read Rev. 21—New Heaven and New Jerusalem

In a few words, describe God, heaven and God's people.

_____

_____

LESSON 30 SUMMARY

GLORIFICATION AND OVERCOMING EVIL

REVELATION

Christ Is Victorious!

God ends the Bible story with Christ's return in full glory, in victorious defeat of Satan. Christ dominates the book of Revelation— the Lamb *"as though it had been slain"* (Rev. 5), and the Warrior who goes forth to conquer and rule, whose name is *"The Word of God,"* (Rev. 19).

Christ demonstrated encouragement through letters to seven churches with evaluation of their faith (Rev. 2-3). We are then shown ever-worsening persecution of the church by Satan and his evil ones (Rev. 4-11). Christ—the Servant Leader and Savior—steps in and battles evil for His believers (Rev. 12-19). The most important fact is in Christ's final victory over Satan and all evil.

CONSIDER how many Christians think of Revelation as too scary, too hard to understand, or too confusing—with the various views of the church age and the 1000 years. But also consider how God gives us the best news of the entire Bible in this book that illustrates visibly Christ's victorious defeat of Satan and all evil from the earth. Consider how this ending of the Bible story is really a beginning of the assurance of our faith that rests on Christ's defeat of Satan on the cross—for our salvation—

and at His second coming—for our resurrected glorification in eternity with God! Praises for the good news that our righteousness is sealed in this hope and assurance of Christ's victories over Satan and all evil!

John Commissioned for a Vision and Revelation

The apostle John was commissioned by Jesus Christ for all generations to follow to give His vision of judgment and the resurrected and glorified Christ (Rev. 1). He wrote, *"The revelation of Jesus Christ, which God gave him to show to his servants the things that must soon take place. He made it known by sending his angel to his servant John, who bore witness to the word of God and to the testimony of Jesus Christ, even to all that he saw,"* (Rev. 1:1-2).

John had been exiled on the island of Patmos because of his witness of Christ (Rev. 1:9). The Roman emperor Domitian had statues built throughout the empire, and called himself *"savior," "lord,"* and even *"god."* Christians, for whom there was only one God (Ex. 20), and one Lord (1 Cor. 8:6) refused to participate in this idolatry, and consequently suffered severe persecution—in many cases, death.

John scribed this picturesque and hopeful book, stressing the Lordship of Christ, the sovereignty of God, and His final victory over all sin and evil. This writing is about things he heard and saw in the revelation granted him by Christ (Rev. 1-2, 19-22).

There are various views about the progression of the revelations and their revealed timing. Whatever view is taken, the practical purpose was—and is—to strengthen the courage and faith of Christians in the face of Christ's coming return. The two general interpretations are: first, that the "1000 years" is a figurative period of time from the church beginning at Pentecost until all saints are glorified in heaven; or second, that the "1000 years" is an exact period at the height of the intense progression of battle culminating at Christ's second coming.

Either way, Christ assures us that, *"Blessed is the one who reads aloud the words of this prophecy, and blessed are those who hear, and who keep what is written in it, for the time is near,"* (Rev. 1:3).

Churches Will Be Compared and People Judged

These Asian churches of John's time, as all churches over time, experienced varied successes and failures (Rev. 2-3). The Ephesian church was commended for its hard work and perseverance, rebuked for forsaking its love for Christ, and called to repent (Rev. 2:1-7). Those at Smyrna were commended for suffering trials and poverty, and called not to fear and have a stronger faith (Rev. 2:8-11).

Pergamum was commended for a true faith, rebuked for compromising doctrines, and called to repent (Rev. 2:12-17). Thyatira was commended for their love, faith, and service. They were rebuked for immorality, and called to repent (Rev. 2:18-29). Sardis was commended for having an effective, yet superficial ministry. They were called to wake up and repent (Rev. 3:1-6). Philadelphia was called faithful with no rebuke, and encouraged to hold onto their faith (Rev. 3:7-13). Laodicea had no commendations, was described as lukewarm, and called to be earnest and repent (Rev. 3:14-22).

Sinful Evil is Punished; Christ Defeats Satan

Christ dominates the Revelation visions—the Lamb *"as though it had been slain"* (Rev. 5), but ever-increasing sin and persecution faces the church and all mankind. The prophetic timeline includes progressive cycles of God's judgment by wrath on sin and evil (Rev. 6-16).

John watched as God gave a scroll with seven seals to the worthy Lamb, Jesus Christ (Rev. 6). Of these seals, as the first four were opened riders appeared on horses of different colors—war, famine, disease, and death were in their path. In between Christ and Satan were war and hunger. When the fifth seal was opened, John saw those in heaven who had been martyred for their faith in Christ. Contrasting images appeared with the sixth seal (Rev. 7). On one side there was a huge earthquake with stars falling from the sky, and on the other multitudes were before God in worship. Finally the seventh seal was opened, unveiling God's judgments with seven trumpets. This shows the defeat of Satan, with God's mighty victory (Rev. 8-19). The visions shift to show the downfall of nations and evil leaders (Rev. 17-18), Christ's triumphant victories (Rev. 19), Christ's judgment over

Satan (Rev. 20), and finally God's new universe (Rev. 21-22). We are shown a glorious worship in heaven with all of God's saints.

Christ Is Victorious!

Christ is once and for all victorious over evil (Rev. 19-20), giving complete hope and assurance to all believers. John wrote, *"After this I heard what seemed to be the loud voice of a great multitude in heaven, crying out, 'Hallelujah! Salvation and glory and power belong to our God, for his judgments are true and just; for he has judged the great prostitute who corrupted the earth with her immorality, and has avenged on her the blood of his servants.'*

Once more they cried out, 'Hallelujah! The smoke from her goes up forever and ever.' And the twenty-four elders and the four living creatures fell down and worshiped God who was seated on the throne, saying, 'Amen. Hallelujah!' And from the throne came a voice saying, 'Praise our God, all you his servants, you who fear him, small and great," (Rev. 19:1-5).

With Satan defeated, John wrote, *"And he who was seated on the throne said, 'Behold, I am making all things new.' Also he said, 'Write this down, for these words are trustworthy and true.' And he said to me, 'It is done! I am the Alpha and the Omega, the beginning and the end. To the thirsty I will give from the spring of the water of life without payment. The one who conquers will have this heritage, and I will be his God and he will be my son. But as for the cowardly, the faithless, the detestable, as for murderers, the sexually immoral, sorcerers, idolaters, and all liars, their portion will be in the lake that burns with fire and sulfur, which is the second death, '"* (Rev. 21:5-8).

CONSIDER how Jesus finished with an offer, saying, *"The Spirit and the Bride say, 'Come.' And let the one who hears say, 'Come.' And let the one who is thirsty come; let the one who desires take the water of life without price,"* (Rev. 22:17). Praises to our Redeemer for His Kingdom of eternal salvation and glory with God!

LINEAGE TREE—GENESIS TO SAMUEL

Luke 3	**Christ's Geneology**	*approximate*
Gen. 1	**God**	eternal
Gen. 2	**Adam** + Eve = Mankind	4000+? B.C.
Gen. 4	Cain, Abel, **Seth** (+10 generations)	?
Gen. 7	**Noah**	?
Gen. 10	**Shem**, Ham (→Canaan), Japheth (+7 gens.)	?
Gen. 11	**Terah**	d. 2090
Gen. 12	**Abraham**	2166
Gen. 25	Ishmael, **Isaac**	2066
Gen. 37	**Jacob** (becomes Israel→12 sons = 12 tribes), Esau	2006
Gen. 37	Joseph and **Judah** and other 10	1916
Ex. 1	Moses	1526
Josh. 1	Joshua	1466
Ruth 3	(Judah +7 gens. to **Boaz** and Ruth in Judges)	c. 1250
Ruth 4	**Obed**	c. 1160
Matt. 1	**Jesse**	c. 1080
1 Sam. 15	**David**	1011

TEN COMMANDMENTS

"AND GOD SPOKE all these words, saying, 'I am the Lord your God, who brought you out of the land of Egypt, out of the house of slavery.'

1. "You shall have **no other gods** before me.
2. "You shall **not make for yourself a carved image**, or any likeness of anything that is in heaven above, or that is in the earth beneath, or that is in the water under the earth. You shall not bow down to them or serve them, for I the Lord your God am a jealous God, visiting the iniquity of the fathers on the children to the third and the fourth generation of those who hate me, but showing steadfast love to thousands of those who love me and keep my commandments.
3. "You shall **not take the name of the Lord your God in vain**, for the Lord will not hold him guiltless who takes his name in vain.
4. "**Remember the Sabbath day**, to keep it holy. Six days you shall labor, and do all your work, but the seventh day is a Sabbath to the Lord your God. On it you shall not do any work, you, or your son, or your daughter, your male servant, or your female servant, or your livestock, or the sojourner who is within your gates. For in six days the Lord made heaven and earth, the sea, and all that is in them, and rested on the seventh day. Therefore the Lord blessed the Sabbath day and made it holy.
5. "**Honor your father and your mother**, that your days may be long in the land that the Lord your God is giving you.
6. "**You shall not murder.**
7. "**You shall not commit adultery.**
8. "You shall not steal.
9. "**You shall not bear false witness against your neighbor.**
10. "**You shall not covet** your neighbor's house; you shall not covet your neighbor's wife, or his male servant, or his female servant, or his ox, or his donkey, or anything that is your neighbor's," (Exodus 20:1-17)

JUDGES OF ISRAEL

references	judges	service	c. dates
Jud. 3:7-11	Othniel	40 yrs.	1380 B.C.
Jud. 3:12-30	Ehud	80 yrs.	
Jud. 3:31	Shamgar	?	
Jud. 4-5	Deborah, Barak	40 yrs.	
Jud. 6-8:32	Gideon	40 yrs.	
Jud. 10:1-2	Tola	23 yrs.	
Jud. 10:3-5	Jair	22 yrs.	
Jud.11-12:7	Jephthah	6 yrs.	
Jud. 12:8-10	Ibzan	7 yrs.	
Jud. 12	Elon	10 yrs.	
Jud. 12	Abdon	8 yrs.	
Jud. 13-16	Samson	20 yrs.	
1 Sam. 1:1-8	Eli		1107
1 Sam. 1-7	Samuel		1067

PROPHETS AND KINGS OF JUDAH AND ISRAEL

context	prophets	united		c. dates
		Judah	Israel	exiles
1 Sam. 8	**Samuel**	**Saul**		1043 B.C.
1 Sam. 15	**Nathan**	**David**		1011-
1 Kings 1		**Solomon**		971-
1 Kings 11	*Ahijah*		*Jeroboam I*	931-
1 Kings 14	Shemaiah	Rehoboam		931-
1 Kings 14		Abijah		915-
1 Kings 15		Asa		912-
1 Kings 15			*Nadab*	910-
1 Kings 15	*Jehu*		*Baasha*	909-
1 Kings 16			*Elah*	886-
1 Kings 16			*Zimri*	885-
1 Kings 16			*Omri*	885-
1 Kings 16	*Elijah*		*Ahab*	874-
1 Kings 22	*Micaiah*	Jehosophat		870-
2 Kings 1			*Ahaziah*	853-
2 Kings 2	*Elisha*		*Jehoram*	852-
2 Kings 8		Jehoram		849-
2 Kings 8	a prophet	Ahaziah		842-
2 Kings 9	Obadiah		*Jehu*	841-
2 Kings 11	Joel	Q. Athaliah		840-
2 Kings 11		Jehoash		836-
2 Kings 13			*Jehoahaz*	814-
2 Kings 13			*Jehoash*	798-
2 Kings 14		Amaziah		796-
2 Kings 14	*Jonah*		*Jeroboam II*	793-
2 Kings 15		Uzziah		792-
2 Kings 15	*Amos*		*Zechariah*	753-
2 Kings 15			*Shallum*	752-
2 Kings 15			*Menahem*	752-
2 Kings 15			*Pekahiah*	752-
2 Kings 15	Isaiah	Jotham		750-
2 Kings 15	*Hosea*		*Pekah*	742-
2 Kings 16		Ahaz		735-
2 Kings 17			*Hoshea*	*732-722*
2 Kings 18	Micah	Hezekiah		716-
2 Kings 21	*Nahum*	Manasseh		697-
2 Kings 21		Amon		643-
2 Kings 22	Zephaniah	Josiah		641-
2 Kings 23	Jeremiah	Jehoahaz		609-
2 Kings 23	Habakkuk	Jehoiakim		609-
Daniel	Daniel			*605-536*
2 Kings 24		Jehoiachin		598-
2 Kings 24		Zedekiah		*597-586*
Ezekiel	Ezekiel			*597-570*
Haggai	Haggai			520-
Zechariah	Zechariah			515-
Malachi	Malachi			432-425

CHRIST'S LIFE AND GOSPELS

Jesus' key life events	Matthew	Mark	Luke	John
Lineage	1:1-17		3:23-38	
Angel's promise to Mary			1:26-38	
Angel appears to Joseph	1:18-25			
Born in Bethlehem			2:1-7	
Shepherds visit			2:8-20	
With parents to temple, circumcised			2:21-40	
Visitors from East	2:1-2			
Escape to Egypt	2:13-18			
Return to Nazareth	2:19-23			
Speaks with temple teachers			2:41-50	
Baptized by John	3:13-17	1:9-11	3:21-22	
Tempted by Satan in desert	4:1-11	1:12-13	4:1-13	
Clears the temple				2:12-25
Talks to woman at well				4:1-26
Preaches in Galilee	4:12-17	1:14-15	4:14-15	4:43-45
Rejected at Nazareth	13:53-58	6:1-6	4:16-30	
Claims to be God's Son				5:19-30
Brothers and sisters in Nazareth	13:55-56	6:3		
Selects twelve disciples	10:1-4	3:13-19	6:12-16	
Preaches Beatitudes on mountain	5:1-12		6:17-26	
Feeds 5,000	14:13-21	6:30-44	9:10-17	6:1-15
Walks on water	14:22-33	6:45-52		6:16-21
Transfigured on mountain	17:1-13	9:2-13	9:28-36	
Visits Mary and Martha			10:38-42	
Answers hostile accusations			11:14-28	
Religious leaders plot to kill				11:45-57
Predicts His death third time	20:17-19	10:32-34	18:31-34	
Enters Jerusalem on donkey			19:28-44	
Clears temple again	21:12-17	11:15-19	19:45-48	
Religious leaders plot to kill again			22:1-2	
Last Supper, Lord's Supper	26:17-29	14:12-25	22:14-30	
Predicts Peter's denial	26:30-35	14:26-31	22:31-34	13:36-38
Betrayed by Judas and arrested	26:47-56	14:43-52	22:47-53	18:1-11
Sanhedrin Council; Peter denies	26:57-75	14:53-72	22:54-71	18:12-27
Tried before Pilot and Herod	27:11-26	15:2-15	23:1-12	18:28-37
Pilate finds no guilt, approves death	27:24-26	15:14-15	23:13-43	18:38-19:27
Dies on Cross	27:45-50	15:21-32	23:44-49	19:28-37
Laid in tomb	27:57-66	15:42-47	23:50-56	19:38-42
Rises from death	28:1-7	16:1-8	24:1-12	20:1-9
Appears to Mary Magdalene		16:9-11		20:10-18
Appears to believers on road		16:12-13	24:13-35	
Appears to disciples in private			24:36-43	
Talks with Peter				21:15-23
Gives Disciples Great Commission	28:16-20	16:15-18	24:44-49	
Ascends into Heaven		16:19-20	24:50-53	

WRITERS OF GOSPELS, ACTS AND LETTERS

books	writers	nationality, from	about
gospels Matthew	Matthew	Jew, Capernaum	tax collector, Christ's apostle
Mark	Mark	Jew, Jerusalem	missionary, Peter's disciple
Luke *history* Acts	Luke	Greek, Antioch	physician, Paul's disciple
gospel John *letters* 1 John 2 John 3 John Revelation	John	Jew, Bethsaida or Capernaum	fisherman, Christ's apostle
Romans 1 Cor. 2 Cor. Galatians Ephesians Philippians Colossians 1 Thess. 2 Thess. 1 Timothy 2 Timothy Titus Philemon	Paul	Jew, Saul of Tarsus	tentmaker, Christ's apostle
Hebrews	Paul?		written to Hebrews
James	James	Jew, Nazareth	carpenter?, Christ's brother
1 Peter 2 Peter	Peter	Jew, Bethsaida	fisherman, Christ's apostle
Jude	Jude	Jew, Nazareth	carpenter?, Christ's brother

THE BIBLE STUDY GUIDE is dedicated to the Christian service of Dr. Peggy T. Cantwell. In gratitude to the adult education ministries, classes and small groups of Fourth Presbyterian Church, Bethesda, Maryland, and National Presbyterian Church, Washington, DC.

All scripture quoted is *English Standard Version* unless otherwise noted. Some Appendix data are approximate based on best available conforming information.

FORWORD BY DR. LUDER G. WHITLOCK, JR., president emeritus of Reformed Theological Seminary and author of the new book, *Divided We Fall: Overcoming a History of Christian Disunity,* (2017). He was executive director of the *Spirit of the Reformation Study Bible* and served on the editorial council of Eternity Advisory board for the *English Standard Version* of *the Bible.*

ROBIN R. KING, CAE, compiled, edited and revised *The Bible Study Guide* after teaching Genesis-to-Revelation curriculum for over 10 years, and serving as Community Bible Study teaching director, Washington, DC, group for 12 years. He holds degrees in communications and education including Old and New Testament surveys, and completed New Testament Letters courses at Reformed Theological Seminary. He is an elder in the Evangelical Presbyterian Church, a fellow and former board member of the C.S. Lewis Institute, and former board president of the Institute for Classical Schools. He has held several non-profit executive roles as CEO, VP, board member, and foundation executive.

EDITORIAL REVIEW: Kent D. Talbert and Carol H. King. COVER: Peter M. King. PUBLISHED BY: the Bible Study Organization, Robin R. King, Editor.